MW00909200

beautifully
WHOLE

authorHOUSE®

KIMBERLY JONES-POTHIER

AuthorHouse™
1663 Liberty Drive
Bloomington, IN 47403
www.authorhouse.com
Phone: 1 (800) 839-8640

Published by AuthorHouse 08/25/2017

ISBN: 978-0-6929-3090-8 (sc)
ISBN: 978-1-5462-0545-6 (e)

Library of Congress Control Number: 2017912989

Printed in the USA

This book is printed on acid-free paper.

New King James Version (NKJV)
Scripture taken from the New King James Version®. Copyright ©
1982 by Thomas Nelson. Used by permission. All rights reserved.

New Living Translation (NLT)
Holy Bible, New Living Translation, copyright © 1996, 2004, 2015
by Tyndale House Foundation. Used by permission of Tyndale House
Publishers Inc., Carol Stream, Illinois 60188. All rights reserved.

The Message (MSG)
Copyright © 1993, 1994, 1995, 1996, 2000,
2001, 2002 by Eugene H. Peterson

Dedication

I would like to dedicate this journal to the
One who has given me more favor than
I deserve, my Lord Jesus Christ!

To each pastor and church who has allowed me
to become a part of your family and my social
media followers who have, without realizing it,
helped to create an international platform where
I am honored to share my love for Christ!

To my amazing church family, Church of the Harvest,
Fayetteville, Georgia, who speaks into my life and
has a consistent prayer covering over me as I travel.

And to my family, the greatest support
system anyone could desire. I could not do
what I do without your love and support.

Acknowledgments

I dedicate this work of love
to my mom, Ann Jones, who has
been my partner in writing
my heart to those who mean the world to me, my
friends. You are my hero!

Contents

Introduction xi

Day 1: Beautifully Broken 1

Day 2: Shine Baby, Shine 6

Day 3: Rejection is God's Protection 11

Day 4: Shake, Rattle & Roll 16

Day 5: Break Through the Brokenness 21

Day 6: Don't Live Out Your Labels 26

Day 7: No Matter What 31

Day 8: From Struggle to Freedom 36

Day 9: You Have the Victory 41

Day 10: Stop Bleeding, and Lead 47

Day 11: Let Go and Walk in Forgiveness 52

Day 12: God Will Use Your Mess 57

Day 13: There is No Surprise With God 62

Day 14: From Pain to Purpose 67

Day 15: *Pursue your Passion* 72

Day 16: *Living in Your Purpose* 77

Day 17: *Get Up, Get Out* 82

Day 18: *Never Go Back* 87

Day 19: *Trust God* 92

Day 20: *Faith over Fear* 97

Day 21: *Sometimes Life Just Happens* 102

Day 22: *Hit Pause and Trust the Process* 107

Day 23: *Delays Aren't Denials* 112

Day 24: *Relax, Let Go and Let God* 117

Day 25: *God is Still Over All* 122

Day 26: *Here Come the Dreamers* 127

Day 27: *Moving On* 132

Day 28: *Heaven Knows Your Name* 137

Day 29: *A Place Called Process* 142

Day 30: *Let It Go* 147

Day 31: *It's Time to Reset* 153

About the Author 159

Introduction

Since the release of my book, "Beautifully Broken," I have traveled thousands of miles ministering to hungry hearts who are experiencing brokenness and just trying to cope with life as they see it. Those who attend my meetings are hungry for change - change in character, change in lifestyle, change in relationships, just change!

Because I can only spend a short time in my meetings giving away what God has given to me, the Lord inspired me to write a life-changing monthly journal that you can use daily to help you not cope with your challenges but defeat those challenges to become victorious through Christ!

Vulnerability is the key to all healing! God is a God of restoration. His redemption plan for your life is greater than anything you have left behind. He turns scars into stars. He uses your mess for your message, and your test for your testimony. The people with the worst past can create the best futures. All you need is a made up mind.

Are you ready? By the time you complete this thirty-one-day journey, God will do an Ephesians 3:20 miracle in your life. One thing I have discovered in life is that it all begins with a mind shift. Until your mind becomes focused on what God says about you instead of what others say about you, you will stay stuck in the present moment. Don't allow a season in your life to define your whole lifetime. Everything you have experienced is part of your life college and you don't have to pay Fannie Mae back a dime. Decide now that you will be powerful instead of pitiful. I feel your victory suddenly is on its way. You must break through in order to have a break through.

Say this prayer with me:

> *"Lord Jesus, open up my mind. I give you permission to change my perception of life and life's challenges. Give me the courage to let go of anything and everything that has been holding me back. I want to be a "water walker." I want to be a comeback kid. Let there be no limitations to your plan for my life. Don't let me downgrade my dreams to match my reality, instead, let me upgrade my faith to match my destiny. No limits, no boundaries, and nothing but increase will surround me. Amen."*

For I know the thoughts that I think toward you, says the Lord, thoughts of peace and not of evil, to give you a future and a hope.

Jeremiah 29:11

Day 1

Beautifully Broken

 *Beautifully Broken... Where God does His best work!*

I will praise You, for I am fearfully and wonderfully made; Marvelous are Your works, and that my soul knows very well. (Psalm 139:14)

THOUGHT FOR TODAY: Identify Your Brokenness!

QUESTION TO CONSIDER: How has your relationship with Jesus Christ helped you to better cope with your brokenness?

Coping means to face and deal with responsibilities, problems or difficulties in a calm or adequate manner. The best way to cope is to take back authority over each of life's challenges by meditating on the written word of God through prayer.

You have not strayed too far to hear God in your life.

Everyone goes through seasons of stillness where the Father seems silent; remember that it is in this silence that His words resonate the loudest.

ILLUSTRATION: A man found a cocoon of an emperor moth and took it home so he could watch the moth come out of the cocoon. One day a small opening appeared. The man sat and watched the moth for several hours as it struggled to force its body through that little hole. Then it seemed to stop making any progress.

To the man it appeared as if the moth had gotten as far as it could in breaking out of the cocoon and was stuck.

Out of kindness, the man decided to help the moth. He took a pair of scissors and snipped off the remaining bit of the cocoon so that the moth could get out. Soon the moth emerged, but it had a swollen body and small-shriveled wings. The man continued to watch the moth, expecting that in time the wings would enlarge and expand to be able to support the body, which would simultaneously, contract to its proper size. Neither happened. In fact, that little moth spent the rest of its life crawling around with a swollen body and shriveled wings. It was never able to fly.

The man in his kindness didn't understand that the restricting cocoon and the struggle required for the moth to get through the tiny opening were God's way of forcing fluid from the body into the wings so that the moth would be ready for flight once it achieved its freedom from the cocoon.

Just as the moth could only achieve freedom and flight as a result of struggling, we often need to struggle to become all that God intends for us to be.

Sometimes, we wish that God would remove our struggles and take away all the obstacles, but just as the man crippled the emperor moth, so would we be crippled if God did that for us. God doesn't take away our problems and difficulties, but He promises to be with us in the midst of them and to use them to restore us- making us into better, stronger people.

 Sit quietly and hear what God is saying to you.

QUESTION TO CONSIDER: How are you conquering your brokenness?

The Bible is full of promises to refute the lies of the enemy. God also has given us spiritual weapons to fight against these spiritual attacks on our emotions. With these weapons, you take authority over your emotions today.

You are fighting for your family and friends. You do not fight against your flesh but those spirits that try to rule and reign in your life.

> *For we wrestle not against flesh and blood, but against principalities, against powers, against the rulers of the darkness of this world, against spiritual wickedness in places. (Ephesians 6:12)*

When you are facing a situation that you cannot seem to find a way out by yourself, turn it over to God.

When you feel as though you have hit a wall in life and cannot go any farther, remember what David said:

> *For by thee I have run through a troop: by my God have I leaped over a wall. (2 Samuel 22:30)*

David was only one example. Most of the leaders used as examples in the Bible went through challenging times, were broken, but came forth as pure gold. They never dreamed that 2,000 years later, we would be calling out their names as examples.

Esther never dreamed there would be movies, books, and sermons about her choice to go before the king for her people. She just faced her fear and did it anyway!

Face your fear and do it anyway!

TODAY'S PRAYER: *Say this prayer loud enough for the devil to hear and write down what God says to you.*

"Lord Jesus, help me to trust in your unfailing love and cause my heart to rejoice in your deliverance. Teach me Your ways and draw me to Your will. Show me the wonders of Your great love and help me to express that love in serving others. You said I am fearfully and wonderfully made so today I choose to release my brokenness and invite You to restore me to wholeness. I decree and declare, "I am more than a conqueror. I am who God says I am. I am no longer a victim but a victor." Amen.

Prayer Reflections:

_____

_____

_____

_____

_____

_____

_____

_____

Day 2

Shine Baby, Shine

 Christians are like glow sticks; they must be broken in order to shine.

For God, who commanded the light to shine out of darkness, hath shined in our hearts, to give the light of the knowledge of the glory of God in the face of Jesus Christ. (2 Corinthians 4:6)

THOUGHT FOR TODAY: You are God's Masterpiece!

QUESTION TO CONSIDER: What does it mean to be broken before God?

On the outside many people will appear as though their life is perfect, never willing to expose their pain. We don't like to talk about overcoming because that means we must tell others that we have experienced pain.

When we suffer, we want God to immediately take away our pain, but sometimes He can be agonizingly slow in answering the problems that we bring to His attention. Even though He may be late with His assistance, I would like to say He is always right on time.

It is in His presence where your brokenness is revealed. Presenting your broken pieces allows Him to penetrate and shine through you.

ILLUSTRATION: *Look at Mary, Martha and their brother, Lazarus, as told in John 11. The members of this little family were among Jesus' closest friends at the time of his earthly ministry. In fact, verse 5 says Jesus loved Mary, Martha and Lazarus.*

One day, Lazarus became very ill, to the point of death. His sisters did the logical thing and sent an urgent message to Jesus saying, "The one you love is sick."

They had every reason to believe that He would immediately respond. However, days had passed before Jesus finally made it to Lazarus, and by that time, it was too late. He had already died. On Jesus' arrival, we read that Martha came to Jesus and said, "If you had been here, my brother would not have died."

Do you think Martha was discouraged because Jesus was too late? Could she have been annoyed when He showed up because she expected Him to be there for them? She may have been tempted to say, "Where have you been Sir? You're too late now. You could have saved him. But apparently there were more important things on your mind."

Do we at times get angry at God because of His delayed timing?

In verse 43, Jesus performed one of His most dramatic miracles as He called Lazarus out of the tomb. You see, Jesus was not late at all. He only appeared to be overdue. He arrived at the precise moment necessary to fulfill the purposes of God, just as He always does.

 *Speak to the Lord about
your brokenness*

QUESTION TO CONSIDER: In what areas of your life have you experienced brokenness?

God's purpose was fulfilled through Lazarus because we read in verse 45 that because of the miracle, many Jews put their faith in Jesus. God is never late when it comes to handling our painful situations. He is always on time.

If Jesus can raise Lazarus from the dead, He can surely work a miracle in your life, if you just believe.

You have been called to be the light of this world. Just like glow sticks, Christians that allow themselves to be broken shine brighter in darkness. Although you have been broken by people, life and circumstances, God can still use you. He has the best redemption plan on the planet for your life.

> *And we know that all things work together for good to those who love God, to those who are the called according to His purpose. (Romans 8:28)*

> *³ And not only that, but we also glory in tribulations, knowing that tribulation produces perseverance; ⁴ and perseverance, character; and character, hope. (Romans 5:3-4)*

God will break your spirit to save your soul. It is never comfortable being broken but it is necessary. God has placed everything on the inside of you to fight off the feelings of defeat and pain. Do not get so familiar with the limp that you walk around broken instead of being whole.

> *But God demonstrates His own love toward us, in that while we were still sinners, Christ died for us. (Romans 5:8)*

TODAY'S PRAYER: *As you pray, proceed with faith that a life change is here.*

Lord Jesus, You said you are near to those who have a broken heart. It does not matter what has come to break me, all things are working together for my good. Today, I am giving you my broken pieces to be used for your glory. I am fearfully and wonderfully made and I decree and declare that today is a new day in Jesus Christ! Amen.

Prayer Reflections:

_____

_____

_____

_____

_____

_____

_____

_____

Day 3

Rejection is God's Protection

 Rejection wasn't someone necessarily wanting me out of their life, but someone that God needed out of my future.

He came to His own, and His own did not receive Him. (John 1:11)

THOUGHT FOR TODAY: Rejection is a gift!

QUESTION TO CONSIDER: Think of a time when you have been rejected. How did you handle that rejection?

There are times we feel people have left us out when it was God who kept us out. Open doors are great but thank God for the closed doors also. No one wants to experience the feeling of being rejected, especially by those whom we love. However, rejection is necessary for your growth.

Some people in our lives are seasonal while others are for a lifetime. Use your discernment to determine who is here just for today and who is here to stay.

Are you being rejected or protected?

Being single or being married doesn't make a difference when it comes to rejection. It is just a matter of what you are going to choose to believe in that particular situation. Whether it's a dating situation, parent or friend, your feelings of rejection do not change the truth of what God says about you or who you are. You must keep in mind that Jesus knew what it felt like to be rejected by His own people and even His disciples. The fact is when you look at it scripturally; God's perfect plan came to fruition because of the rejections Jesus encountered. Did Jesus feel sorry for himself while asking people why they did not like Him? Preposterous! He was about the Father's business. In doing so, He walked in the knowledge that He was a Son fully accepted and secure in His Father's provision. The next time your feelings of rejection surface, ask God to reveal His truths to you.

> *Never will I leave you, never will I forsake you. (Hebrews 13:5)*

ILLUSTRATION: *In Genesis 37, Joseph was only 17 years of age when his brothers threw him into the pit and then sold him to Egyptian merchants. He felt abandoned as* *he was sold to Potipher and then sent to prison because of a lie. Joseph went through more rejection in a short time than most of us experience in a lifetime. He was a living example of a godly man through every encounter. Because of Joseph's heart posture, he not only forgave his brothers but was able to save his entire family during the worst famine in the history of the nation. This Jewish boy became second in command in Egypt to Pharaoh and watched God give him favor in every season of his life.*

How can one young man like Joseph flourish in the midst of adversity when adversity meets him in every area of his life? Remember that God shows no partiality. This means we all will go through trials and yet, we too can stand as Joseph stood. You will have friends and even family members turn against you, however you too can affirm that your God will keep you.

 How can you allow rejection in your life to be a stepping stone to your future?

QUESTION TO CONSIDER: How can you move on after much rejection?

The toughest rejection to move forward from is that of family. If you were abandoned as a child, abused or treated differently, God loves you abundantly. He has a great future planned for your life.

Even if my father and mother abandon me, the Lord will hold me close. (Psalms 27:10, NLT)

Many times we hold onto a relationship well past its season. God will do for you what you would not have ever done for yourself. You see, He sees your future and knows those who are creating havoc in your life now will not be able to go to your next level.

Many times these relationships are distractions. The people God have assigned to be a part of your life will believe in you, love you and support you.

They push you to breakthroughs and not breakdowns.

Remember, sometimes the person you want does not deserve you. Just because someone looks good doesn't mean they are good for you.

Although people conspire against you, look at what God transpires in you.

Do not give up! God will give you back two-fold for every tear that was shed and every regret that comes to mind.

TODAY'S PRAYER: *Take a moment, release your pain and allow God to speak to you.*

Lord Jesus, I am ready and willing to accept your divine protection in my life. I know I am valuable and precious to you Lord. Even when so many walk away, You have never turned your back on me. You said You would never leave me nor forsake me. I take You at Your Word! Help me to survive and thrive! Amen.

Prayer Reflections:

_____

_____

_____

_____

_____

_____

_____

_____

_____

_____

Day 4

Shake, Rattle & Roll

 Shake off rejection and realize it's for your protection.

Count yourself blessed every time someone cuts you down or throws you out, every time someone smears or blackens your name to discredit me. What it means is that the truth is too close for comfort and that, that person is uncomfortable. You can be glad when that happens—skip like a lamb, if you like!—for even though they don't like it, I do . . . and all heaven applauds. And know that you are in good company; my preachers and witnesses have always been treated like this. (Luke 6:22-23 MSG)

THOUGHT FOR TODAY: Let go of the wrong people!

QUESTION TO CONSIDER: What area in your life have you felt the most rejection?

Rejection is a tough pill to swallow, but not only is it God's protection but His redirection as well. We all desire to be loved, accepted and appreciated. When you do not get that validation, escort those people to the balcony of your life and allow them to only watch you from a distance.

Praise is always birthed out of rejection.

If you haven't been through anything, you will not know how to praise. If you have been through hell, your next birth must be praise.

One thing that would make life so much easier is for you to stop putting pressure on yourself to be perfect by measuring yourself to the world's standards. It actually seems that you lose yourself with each failure.

Failure is not failure unless you quit trying.

Have you ever asked yourself, "So what happens if the worst thing I ever imagined happened to me?" If you haven't, maybe you should. It allows you to realize that the thing that you worry about happening to you can't affect you. Yes, it may set you back. You may have to start over. You may feel lost. You may take a little time to heal. But so what?

I have found that even in my worst season of

adversity, it was the greatest blessing in my life, and that most of the time we, as people, live our lives running away from something that isn't even after us.

It is a shame that you would allow your pride and fear of failure and what others think of you to keep you trapped in a world of worry, fear and fake personas just because you don't want others to judge you.

I challenge you to shake yourself loose from trying to fix your past to the point that you cannot even live in your future.

If your dream has been shattered into hundreds of pieces, do not be afraid to pick one up and start over again. It may turn out to be a masterpiece.

 Take an inventory of your past rejections and release them.

QUESTION TO CONSIDER: How are you now equipped to accept rejection as God's protection?

Never beg people to see the good in you!

You just do you and let your life reveal your gift. Believe in yourself. God already sees your potential. God loves you too much to leave you the way you are. He wants what is best for you even if it costs Him the life of His only begotten Son. Jesus came so that you might have life and that more abundantly.

The thief does not come except to steal, and to kill and to destroy, I have come that they may have life, and that they may have it more abundantly (John 10:10)

Walking through rejection is almost as painful as being rejected. You can and will get through the pain because God will restore your life with the right people, at the right time, for the right reasons.

ILLUSTRATION: *In Daniel 3 there were three Hebrew men, Shadrach, Meshach and Abednego who were guilty only of worshiping the one true God. King Nebuchadnezzar made a huge golden statue, ninety feet high and nine feet wide and commanded everyone in the kingdom to bow down and worship the golden image. Everyone bowed down except Shadrach, Meshach and Abednego and as a result were rejected by everyone because they would not conform to the king's ways. They were then thrown into the fiery furnace because they would not bow down and forsake their God. These men were young but even in the face of rejection and fear, they chose to stand. The end of the story is that God sent a fourth person into that furnace that day to protect those men. You can also stand and know that God is fighting for you.*

TODAY'S PRAYER: *Accept what the Word of God says about you.*

Lord Jesus, I am your beloved child. I am safe and secure in Your hands. Thank you for accepting me unconditionally. Thank you for turning people's rejection of me into your protection. Help me not only to fully accept how much You love me, but help me to abide in Your love. I have the assurance of Your word that You will restore me and make me strong, firm and steadfast. Amen.

Prayer Reflections:

_____

_____

_____

_____

_____

_____

_____

_____

_____

_____

Day 5

Break Through the Brokenness

 You've been in this place long enough. It's time to arise! Your breakthrough is breaking forth. There is a miracle with your name on it!

And the peace of God, which surpasses all understanding, will guard your hearts and minds through Christ Jesus. (Philippians 4:7)

THOUGHT FOR TODAY: God wants to restore you!

QUESTION TO CONSIDER: How will you allow God to help you escape your brokenness?

The enemy will always try to control your mind by forcing you to live a life of oppression and depression. He will cause you to rehearse those memories of hurt, shame, anger and defeat and you will want to give up.

You will feel like a turtle stuck in peanut butter, not able to move forward.

You just get up, help God help you to break through the brokenness. You need to know it is God's will to heal you. One of the hindrances of your ability to receive from God is the way you see Him. If you don't know or trust someone, your ability to have faith in him is greatly diminished. God's word tells us that you must believe in faith as you approach Him.

> But without faith it is impossible to please Him, for he who comes to God must believe that He is, and that He is a rewarder of those who diligently seek Him. (Hebrews 11:6)

Jesus freely healed all who came to Him and instructed His disciples to do the same. You are praying for a miracle but expecting defeat. How do you expect a miracle when you are not willing to break through? You must prepare for what you are praying. God is not a genie in a bottle. Help Him help you. You may be depressed but you must decide to keep going. When you receive a doctor's negative report, whose report are you going to believe?

You shall live and not die. You must put one foot in front of the other. It may be slow movement but at least you are moving forward. You may be down today but you will be up tomorrow. With God, it always works out in the end.

If it hasn't worked out, it's not the end. There is no shame when you stumble.

ILLUSTRATION: *Have you seen a palm tree in a hurricane? That tree may be bent so far over that it is almost touching the ground. When the wind finally stops, the palm tree bounces right back up. What is interesting is that, while the palm tree is bent over during the pressure of the storm, it is actually growing stronger. Psalm 92:12 tells us that the righteous shall flourish like a palm tree. The reason God said we would flourish like a palm tree is because He knew there would be difficult times. He knew challenges would come against you and try to steal your joy and victory. God said you would be like a palm tree because when the storms of life blow, you will be stronger than before.*

Think on the challenges you have faced in which God has delivered you.

QUESTION TO CONSIDER: What decisions can you make today that will change your life for the better tomorrow?

It is so much easier allowing Jesus Christ to direct your steps rather than continuing to make your own path. When you decide you no longer want to live broken, God is right there ready to give you direction. When you receive Jesus Christ as Lord, you receive more than you can imagine.

I will never forget the night that I finally got sick and tired of being sick and tired of my situation, of my pain.

After begging God to take away all the hurt, He gently said to me, "I can't take it, you have to give it to me." That moment was life changing for me. I had been allowing the 'what ifs' of life to totally rule me; however, that night something changed.

I did not know how to forgive so I asked God to show me how to let all the hurt and pain go. I then began forgiving everyone that had ever hurt me because I was ready to be free. I had no idea it would set me up for a change that would propel me into the ministry that I am in today.

There was purpose in my pain.

> *No weapon formed against you shall prosper, And every tongue which rises against you in judgment You shall condemn. This is the heritage of the servants of the Lord, And their righteousness is from Me," Says the Lord. (Isaiah 54:17)*

DAILY PRAYER: *Give up as you pray and allow Jesus to be Lord of every situation.*

Lord Jesus, thank you for opening my eyes to the tactics used by the enemy to control my actions. I will allow You to direct my steps and cause me to be at peace with my family and friends. I will walk in forgiveness and will not allow the pain of my past to rule me. I refuse to stay the same. Amen.

Prayer Reflections:

_____

_____

_____

_____

_____

_____

_____

_____

_____

_____

_____

_____

Day 6

Don't Live Out Your Labels

God is delivering you so you no longer need to accept/conform to the cardboard box that people have placed you in- decorating it and calling it 'home'.

¹ *And He entered the synagogue again, and a man was there who had a withered hand.* ² *So they watched Him closely, whether He would heal him on the Sabbath, so that they might accuse Him.* ³ *And He said to the man who had the withered hand, "Step forward."* ⁴ *Then He said to them, "Is it lawful on the Sabbath to do good or to do evil, to save life or to kill?" But they kept silent.* ⁵ *And when He had looked around at them with anger, being grieved by the hardness of their hearts, He said to the man, "Stretch out your hand." And he stretched it out, and*

his hand was restored as whole as the other.
(Mark 3:1-5)

THOUGHT FOR TODAY: No longer allow people to determine your worth!

QUESTION TO CONSIDER: How have labels limited your identity?

Labels take away your value and limit your potential. They replace your true identity in Christ with false identities. When you allow your labels to identify who you are, then you are functioning within the confines of the label. Get to know who you are in Christ!

We tend to find our identity in labels.

We assume that what has always been, will always be. My husband treated me like I am less than, so I must be less than. My father molested me so I guess I deserved it. My mother abandoned me so I'm not worthy of true love. We willingly adopt the labels with the struggles such as anger, bitterness, unforgiveness, failure, or addiction.

> *I have been crucified with Christ. It is no longer I who live, but Christ who lives in me. (Galatians 2:20)*

Paul was saying that when his old self died, all the

labels given by others also died. This is true for you today. When you give your heart to Jesus Christ and accept Him as Lord and Savior, you are transformed into a new creature. The old things are passed away and you now begin a brand new life in Christ.

ILLUSTRATION: In John 18:15-27, after denying Jesus three times, Peter wept bitterly knowing that he had done the very thing he said he would never do! He had repentance in his heart and yet knew he failed his Lord. Remember when Jesus was resurrected? He sent a personal message to his disciples, including Peter, that He had risen. Jesus knew Peter's heart. He knew he had a repentant spirit. He would not always be known as a traitor. Jesus knew Peter would be the main speaker on the day of Pentecost to 3,000 believers in Jerusalem. Jesus saw Peter's worth. He saw Peter's faults as well, but accepted Peter as he was, knowing his heart was good. It has been said that our choices determine our circumstances, and our decisions determine our destiny.

What is holding you back? What is delaying your decision to surrender those labels and choose to change?

QUESTION TO CONSIDER: What labels have you given yourself and how has that impacted your life?

Some people wear self-imposed labels like "I'm not smart enough or pretty enough." Contrary to what most believe, being saved does not erase the pain or the memory of what happened to you. Instead it gives you a place of safety to walk out forgiveness.

This is important for you today.

You are only who or what you answer to, and who you are is not what you have done or what was done to you.

When you know who God has called you to be, you will not answer to anything less than that name. No longer answer to what happened to you because God has called you His; you are His child and He is your Father.

> *Even before he made the world, God loved us and chose us in Christ to be holy and without fault in his eyes. (Ephesians 1:4 NLT)*

> *[17] How precious are your thoughts about me, O God. They cannot be numbered! [18] I can't even count them; they outnumber the grains of sand! And when I wake up, you are still with me! (Psalm 139:17-18)*

Don't let the ugly lies that people say about you destroy God's truth about you.

Every day you must live in light of who you truly

are. When you are tempted to be angry, remember that anger belongs to the old you. When you are tempted to lust, remember that lust belongs to your old self. When you are tempted to worry, remember that your old, worrying self was crucified with Christ. You are not your labels.

DAILY PRAYER: *Allow the Holy Spirit to reveal His presence to you.*

Lord Jesus, I will not allow a disability or label to become my identity today. I decree and declare that before You made the world, You loved me and chose me in Christ to be holy and without fault in Your eyes. When I wake up or lay down, You are always with me.

Prayer Reflections:

_____

_____

_____

_____

_____

_____

_____

Day 7

No Matter What

> *God wants your next thing*
> *to be your best thing!*

¹ Now it came to pass, in the days when the judges ruled, that there was a famine in the land. And a certain man of Bethlehem, Judah, went to dwell in the country of Moab, he and his wife and his two sons. ² The name of the man was Elimelech, the name of his wife was Naomi, and the names of his two sons were Mahlon and Chilion—Ephrathites of Bethlehem, Judah. And they went to the country of Moab and remained there. ³ Then Elimelech, Naomi's husband, died; and she was left, and her two sons. ⁴ Now they took wives of the women of Moab: the name of the one was Orpah, and the name of the other Ruth. And they dwelt there about ten years. ⁵ Then both Mahlon and Chilion also died; so the woman survived her two sons and her husband. ... ¹¹ But Naomi said, "Turn back, my daughters; why will you go with me? Are there still sons in my womb, that they may be your husbands? ... ¹⁶ But Ruth said: "Entreat me not to leave you, Or to turn back from following after you; For wherever you go, I will go; And wherever you lodge, I will lodge; Your people shall be my people, And your God, my God. (Ruth 1:1-5, 11, 16)

THOUGHT FOR TODAY: You have a lot to do with what happens next in your life.

QUESTION TO CONSIDER: How will my beliefs today determine what I receive tomorrow?

When you change your thinking, you change your doing. In this life you must make choices. Some are very important choices. Some are not.

Many of your choices are between good and evil.

The choices you make determine to a large extent your happiness or your unhappiness, because you must live with the consequences of your choices. *Making perfect choices all the time is not possible;* however, it is possible to make choices in which you can live and thrive.

After her husband died, Naomi began to pour all her hopes into her sons and their wives. Ten years later, her sons died.

> *What do you do when your hope has nowhere to go?*

All Naomi had left was her two daughters-in-law, Orpah and Ruth, who were committed to stay with her. As Naomi makes the decision to return to Bethlehem, she encourages Orpah and Ruth to return to Moab with their families. Sometimes when your hope is lost, you try to push people away. Joy is supposed to be contagious, but what do you do when there is no joy left? Orpah returns to her family, however Ruth made the choice to continue with Naomi. The amazing thing about destiny is that just because you start with someone doesn't mean you end up with them. Naomi did not know what her life would become in Bethlehem, but she knew Ruth would be there with her.

 What choices do you need to make to see change in your present state?

QUESTION TO CONSIDER: How can I be faithful with what I have?

Imagine how awkward it must have been when Naomi and Ruth arrived back in Bethlehem. They were comforted by people who had watched Naomi's family leave their city looking for a better place. **Naomi had left full of hope and now she was returning empty and broken.**

Naomi could not promise Ruth a future and yet Ruth would not leave her mother-in-law. Have you ever been through so much that you could not go back to whom you used to be? You sensed the road ahead may be uncertain but you knew going ahead was much better than going back to whom you once were. Ruth faithfully began to serve Naomi as a daughter. She could never have dreamed that eventually she would become the owner of the very field in which she was begging.

When you follow God faithfully no matter what, your next thing will be your best thing. *Even when you are planted, you have storms.*

Serve God faithfully:

1. No matter what has happened in your past, believe that God still has a great plan for your future.
2. No matter what, believe that who you are aligned with is more important than where you have been.
3. No matter what, believe that faithfulness matters.

DAILY PRAYER: *Grasp faith that God will set you at the right place and the right time.*

Lord Jesus, I am determined to be the vessel you created me to be. I will serve those in my life who are in need of assurance and love, and will look for hope even in the midst of life's storms. Lord, I will not waver through unbelief regarding Your promises, but I desire to be strengthened in my faith and give You glory while being fully persuaded that You have power to do what You promise. I realize the qualities of the faithful are honor, consistency and loyalty. Amen.

Prayer Reflections:

_____

_____

_____

_____

_____

_____

_____

Day 8

From Struggle to Freedom

 The life of the godly is not a straight line to glory, but they do get there.

A man's heart plans his way, But the Lord directs his steps. (Proverbs 16:9)

14 Then the women said to Naomi, "Blessed be the Lord, who has not left you this day without a close relative; and may his name be famous in Israel! 15 And may he be to you a restorer of life and a nourisher of your old age; for your daughter-in-law, who loves you, who is better to you than seven sons, has borne him." (Ruth 4:14-15)

THOUGHT FOR TODAY: We cannot recreate our pasts.

QUESTION TO CONSIDER: How can you take your past failures and turn them into freedom?

Whatever has happened in your past has happened. You cannot recreate or reconstruct those situations. In the book of Ruth, we see how Naomi and her husband were full of expectation when they left Bethlehem, the land of famine, for Moab. Naomi never dreamed she would lose her husband and two sons. If possible, she would have recreated her life and made different plans. *With God, whatever has happened in your past need not destroy you.*

The book of Ruth teaches us that God's purpose for the life of His people is to connect us to something far greater than ourselves. God wants us to know that when we follow Him, our lives always mean more than we think they do. Everything we do in obedience to God, no matter how small, is significant. No matter what has happened in your life, with God there is grace, peace and hope, if you run to Him and bring every past failure and disappointment and lay them at His feet.

> *16 But Ruth said: "Entreat me not to leave you, Or to turn back from following after you; For wherever you go, I will go; And wherever you lodge, I will lodge; Your people shall be my people, And your God, my God.*
> *17 Where you die, I will die, And there will I be buried. The Lord do so to me, and more*

also, If anything but death parts you and me." (Ruth 1:16-17)

Ruth stood in stark contrast to both her Moabite background and the failures of Israel during her time. She was a Gentile who began a relationship with the God of Israel even though she was from a heathen nation.

Ruth demonstrated God's grace in that she received blessings she did not merit.

If Ruth was guilty of anything it was being guilty of love. She truly loved her mother-in-law and gave up her life as she knew it for Naomi.

 What choices have you made that created storms in your life that only Jesus could recreate?

QUESTION TO CONSIDER: What expectations have kept you imprisoned and how can you break out to be free?

Life is made up of choices. Many times we fail those closest to us while trying to control our life events; however, it only takes one choice to allow Jesus Christ to be Lord. Naomi could have forced Ruth to return to her family; however, she finally gave up and welcomed her to the journey of life back to Bethlehem.

If God could set the cosmos into order with only a spoken word, He can surely categorize your life.

The story of Ruth is a series of setbacks. Even though Ruth clung to Naomi and returned with her to Bethlehem, Naomi's bitter complaint was, "I went out full and the Lord has brought me back empty. The Almighty has dealt very bitterly with me." Naomi could not imagine a life without pain and loss. She had no idea that God had a plan that was working for her good. She could never dream that the young woman, Ruth, would love her as much as any child could love a mother, would marry Boaz, a rich landowner, and eventually become the great-grandmother of King David and an ancestor of the Messiah.

Naomi never dreamed her grandchild would be in the family lineage of the Lord Jesus Christ. You too have a future and a hope. God gives you a promise in Jeremiah 29:13 that you will seek and find Him when you search for Him with all your heart.

> *[12] Then you will call upon Me and go and pray to Me, and I will listen to you. [13] And you will seek Me and find Me, when you search for Me with all your heart. (Jeremiah 29:12-13)*

Circumstances should never affect the life of a believer. Faith always prevails over circumstance.

DAILY PRAYER: *See God's sovereign plan in your life as you offer up your sacrifice of praise.*

Lord Jesus, as Ruth gave up her life as it was to become the daughter of Naomi, I offer myself up as a living sacrifice, holy and acceptable to You today. I declare that I will walk out the plan You created for me long before I was born. I will see the good in each season of life and allow You to be Lord of all. Lord, give me a determination and willingness to let hurt go, to release mercy and bless those who have hurt me. I will stand on your promise today, practice mercy and surrender each situation to You. Amen.

Prayer Reflections:

_____

_____

_____

_____

_____

_____

_____

Day 9

You Have the Victory

The tide is turning and everything that has been draining you is drying up.

⁹ That is what the Scriptures mean when they say, "No eye has seen, no ear has heard, and no mind has imagined what God has prepared for those who love him." ¹⁰ But it was to us that God revealed these things by his Spirit. For his Spirit searches out everything and shows us God's deep secrets. (1 Corinthians 2:9-10 NLT)

THOUGHT FOR TODAY: Jesus is the solution to all bad news in your life!

QUESTION TO CONSIDER: How can I be free from unhealthy people and bad decisions in my life?

Your attachment to unhealthy people and bad habits, which offer no real control, is why you spiritually die and live a life out of balance.

Pay attention!
You are going to live forever.

Your soul will exist eternally, either in a stage of separation from God, or in eternal life with Him. Your situation today is temporary! It will not last! Know that God sees you and has a purpose for you which He wrote in His book long before you were born!

Keep your heart with all diligence for out of
it spring the issues of life. (Proverbs 4:23)

I look at toxic people like termites. You are busy trying to build an empire while they are busy trying to eat away at the foundation. They want to ride with you in your car as long as you are paying. When the money runs out, their loyalty runs out. These friends are distractions. The truth is you outgrow people just like you outgrow clothes. Be very cautious to not allow people in your life who continually enable a bad habit in which God has set you free.

There is a difference in people who are attached to you and those who are assigned to you.

Someone attached is always clinging to you because they don't have the fortitude to accomplish what you are accomplishing. They will leave you in a second for the next best thing. They are not loyal and will not cover you in crisis. Most likely, they will tell your business to anyone that asks. They usually push you to breakdowns and not breakthroughs. Bringing more chaos and confusion than peace into your life, they do not believe in their own dreams so they want to steal yours. They are dream drainers and joy stealers.

Someone assigned to you is someone God put in your life. This person will remind you where you are headed when it gets tough: someone who has your back when it's not popular to have your back, someone who will believe in your dreams as if they were their own, someone who loves you unconditionally and when you were invisible, and someone who prays for you daily and speaks life into your life. These people would ride with you in the bus and care less if you ever have a limo. They love you for you and could care less if you ever give them anything.

Make a list of five closest friends in your world because they are a prophecy of where you are headed:

QUESTION TO CONSIDER: How can I have the courage to let go of toxic friends in whom I have become codependent?

Each of us have been hurt deeply by toxic people in our lives. There is a difference between letting people go because you've outgrown them and letting them go because you're jaded by them.

Check your heart posture.

Proverbs 4:23 tells you to guard your heart with all diligence. Learn to walk in forgiveness. I firmly believe that as life goes on, there are seasonal people who cannot go with you. However, when it's clear you're outgrowing someone, you do not feel a need to let them know through subliminal messages.

You don't leave them talking about them and trying to hurt them like they hurt you. Just let them go. You know you're in right standing with God when their name is mentioned and your heart doesn't hurt anymore.

My friend, you are free and clear and walking in forgiveness.

I am always amazed how certain groups of people attract each other. Unstable people tend to find unstable people. Lazy people find other lazy people.

Crazy people find other crazy people, and complaining people find other complaining people.

Put a large group of people in a room and eventually, people with the same characteristics, behavioral tendencies, and interests will find each other. Like magnets connecting. Make sure as you finish this devotional that you are attracting the right kind of people.

I would rather have four quarters than one hundred pennies. In my words, one devoted friend who is honest with you is worth ten unstable friends that you cannot count on in time of trouble.

DAILY PRAYER: *Allow this day to be your opportunity for change.*

Lord Jesus, I give you permission to reveal those friends who are attached to me and not assigned to me. Give me the courage to let go, move forward and walk into my destiny with no strings attached. As I release them, I pray blessings over them. I ask you to draw them to you because they cannot come unless you draw them. Allow them to become honest with themselves and honest with you. I truly forgive so I can move forward. Amen.

Prayer Reflections:

_____

_____

_____

_____

_____

_____

_____

_____

_____

_____

_____

_____

_____

_____

_____

_____

_____

_____

_____

_____

Day 10

Stop Bleeding, and Lead

You walked through your mess for a reason!

¹ The Lord is my light and my salvation; whom shall I fear? the Lord is the strength of my life; of whom shall I be afraid? ² When the wicked, even mine enemies and my foes, came upon me to eat up my flesh, they stumbled and fell. ³ Though an host should encamp against me, my heart shall not fear: though war should rise against me, in this will I be confident. ⁴ One thing have I desired of the Lord, that will I seek after; that I may dwell in the house of the Lord all the days of my life, to behold the beauty of the Lord, and to enquire in his temple. ⁵ For in the time of trouble he shall hide me in his pavilion: in the secret of his tabernacle shall he hide me; he shall set me up upon a rock. [6] And now shall mine head be lifted up above mine enemies round about me: therefore will I offer in his tabernacle sacrifices of joy; I will sing, yea, I will sing praises unto the Lord. (Psalms 27:1-6)

THOUGHT FOR TODAY: You cannot endure the race when you do not even begin.

QUESTION TO CONSIDER: How can I walk out the purpose that God has for me even in the middle of challenge?

When you realize that God has a plan for you, it opens your spiritual understanding that He leads, guides and directs your steps. No matter how difficult the challenge, He said He'd never leave nor forsake you. If that person who wounded you took back the pain they caused, you would lose the strength you gained. How cool is it that the same God that created mountains, oceans and galaxies looked at you and thought the world needed one of you too?

How can you trust in God when you don't even trust the God in you?

You don't want to go through the test to pass the test. You hate going through the process. *You want to break generational curses* but you don't want to go through the process to destroy them. You focus so much on the bleeding, you can't get to the promise. If you can't get to the Father during your tired days, you will prolong the process.

You pray on the level you believe.

You receive on the level you believe. If you aren't receiving on a high level, you aren't believing on a high level.

> *Now faith is the substance of things hoped for, the evidence of things not seen. (Hebrews 11:1)*

Stop blaming God for your position. You would be much further along if you endure. The Bible says you will be complete, lacking nothing. You have an inheritance. Don't forget about the blessings. They are rich and have no sorrows. So often you nurse wounds that do not prosper. Remember no weapon formed against you shall prosper. When the enemy comes at you, he has no weapon that can penetrate that faith shield. Stop being afraid of the weapon.

What is the difference between believing for a miracle and hoping for change?

QUESTION TO CONSIDER: How can I walk out my purpose when the enemy tells me I'm not qualified?

> *You saw me before I was born. Every day of my life was recorded in your book. Every moment was laid out before a single day had passed. (Psalm 139:16, NLT)*

If the enemy is fighting you, it is not because you're weak. It's because you are strong. The enemy isn't fighting you for your past or present. He fights for your future! He will bring up every mistake, every failure and will make sure you hear every word from your haters because he cannot touch you physically. The enemy will get you through distractions, through your emotions.

> *And do not be conformed to this world, but be transformed by the renewing of your mind, that you may prove what is that good and acceptable and perfect will of God. (Romans 12:2)*

Allow God to transform your mind. This transformation comes through spending time in His presence. Pay attention to your thought patterns. Wrong thought patterns can cause you to fail. No matter what people have done to you or you have done to yourself, it will not cause you to fail.

Grace forgives us but also gives us the power to overcome.

Give your entire attention to what God is doing right now. Don't get worried about what may or may not happen tomorrow. God will help you deal with whatever challenges come when the time arrives.

DAILY PRAYER: *Believe for a new season.*

Lord Jesus, please give me enough patience to wait on the answers to my prayers. And if what I am asking is not aligned according to Your will, please have Your way. I know that you have better plans for me, much better than I could have for myself. Help me to listen to you in prayer as much as you listen to me. Amen.

Prayer Reflections:

_____

_____

_____

_____

_____

_____

_____

_____

Day 11

Let Go and Walk in Forgiveness

 Having class is the ability to walk away from a bad situation with forgiveness in your heart and a smile on your face.

And whenever you stand praying, if you have anything against anyone, forgive him, that your Father in heaven may also forgive you your trespasses. (Mark 11:25)

THOUGHT FOR TODAY: Forgiveness reflects God's character.

QUESTION TO CONSIDER: Why is forgiveness for you and not for the one who violated you?

Every one of us have been deeply hurt by someone else. It may have been a parent, an ex-spouse, a current mate, a sibling, a former friend, a relative or perhaps a stranger. Maybe a hurt that came from some violent or reckless act. It may have been something that somebody should have done but didn't. It may be something that took place over many years. It may be something that happened in a moment.

Even as you read this devotional, there may be a situation or person that immediately pops into your mind and begins to make your stomach churn. The command in the Bible to forgive is most difficult because *sometimes you don't want to forgive.* You want to strike back. You want justice. You want the other person to know the pain they inflicted. If you can't have justice, you vow that you will never have a relationship with that person again. You avoid and ignore them. It is not surprising that when we talk about forgiveness, we are more interested in finding loopholes than in obeying.

Let's begin with the facts.

Why does God make such an issue of forgiveness? I think we can answer that question several different ways. First, forgiveness reflects God's character, His love. Forgiveness gives us the opportunity to extend to others what God has extended to us. Do you remember where you were when He found you? Can you recall the countless times you ignored God while continuing to do what you knew was wrong?

You had a hard time forgiving even as the Lord reached out to you and offered His forgiveness. When you received His love, He promised He would remember the past no longer. When we forgive, we demonstrate that we have not forgotten where He found us. (But you say, "If we forgive aren't we just letting someone get away with a wrong?") We feel if we simply forgive, we allow that person to take advantage of us. Shouldn't we make people aware of the wrong they have done? The scripture says of a man that it is his glory to pass over a transgress (Proverbs 19:11).

It is more honorable to bury an injury than to avenge it.

But what if the wrong is great? Not forgiving is a greater wrong. Forgiveness releases you!

 Take a second and think about those people who have hurt you that you need to forgive. Give them back the pain they left with you and take back the peace they took from you.

QUESTION TO CONSIDER: When have you truly forgiven?

You have forgiven when you strive against all thoughts of revenge. When you will not do your enemies harm but wish well for them. Forgiveness has truly taken place when past actions no longer hold a present bearing.

True forgiveness takes time.

People who refuse to forgive hurt themselves. Bitter people are no fun to be around. They can't sleep. Ulcers line their stomach. They see the negatives in every situation because their life is polluted with feelings of resentment and anger. People who are unwilling to forgive may feel they are punishing the other person, but *the only person paying the price is himself or herself.*

Try a simple experiment on yourself. Make a fist and hold it tight. One minute of this is sufficient to bring discomfort. Consider what would happen if the fist were maintained in that state of tension during a period that extended over weeks, months or even years. Obviously, it would become a sick member of the body. You may hurt a person by not forgiving them and thus feel some satisfying sense of getting even, but almost without exception, the hurt you do to yourself may be even greater.

After a while you may not feel the pain of the clenched resentment in your soul, but its self-inflicted paralysis will have its affect on your whole life.

The roots of bitterness go deep. The deeper the hurt, the more time may be needed for the difficult work of forgiveness. *Forgiveness is a decision of the mind and the heart that must be reaffirmed over and over.*

DAILY PRAYER: *Ask the Lord to show you where to extend forgiveness today.*

Lord Jesus, show me where I need to extend forgiveness to those who have hurt me. Give me strength to let go and let You work in me. I forgive myself and those who have wrongfully hurt me, knowingly or unknowingly, in Jesus' name. Amen.

Prayer Reflections:

_____

_____

_____

_____

_____

_____

_____

_____

_____

_____

_____

_____

_____

Day 12

God Will Use Your Mess

 Everybody wants to be a diamond,
but nobody wants to get cut!

The younger son told his father, 'I want my
share of your estate now before you die.'
So his father agreed to divide his wealth
between his sons. (Luke 15:12)

THOUGHT FOR TODAY: God will use your mess to qualify you where He is taking you.

QUESTION TO CONSIDER: How can you make the right life decision in the middle of a struggle?

Luke 15 tells us the story of the prodigal son as Jesus identifies Himself with God in His loving attitude to the lost. The younger son symbolized the sinner who was caught up in riotous living. The implication is that the son could not wait for his father's death for his inheritance, he wanted it immediately. The father agrees and divides his estate between both sons.

Both the son's asking and the father's granting of this request would have been shocking to the people of that day. Upon receiving his portion of the inheritance, the younger son travels to a distant country and wastes all his money in extravagant living. Immediately thereafter, a famine strikes the land; he becomes desperately poor and is forced to take work feeding the swine. When he reaches the point of envying the food of the pigs he is watching, he finally comes to his senses.

> *17 And when he came to himself, he said, How many hired servants of my father's have bread enough and to spare, and I perish with hunger! 18 I will arise and go to my father, and will say unto him, Father, I have sinned against heaven, and before thee, 19 And am no more worthy to be called thy son: make me as one of thy hired servants. 20 And he arose, and came to his father. But when he was yet a great way off, his father saw him, and had compassion, and ran, and fell on his neck, and kissed him. (Luke 15:17-20)*

Jesus portrayed the father as waiting for his son,

perhaps daily searching the distant road, hoping for his appearance. The son came to himself in the pigpen feeding the swine after spending his entire inheritance. He decided to return home and repent while asking for mercy. He had no idea that his father would immediately show mercy and extend forgiveness.

The son does not even have time to finish his rehearsed speech, since the father calls for his servants to dress him in a fine robe, a ring, and sandals, and slaughter the "fattened calf" for a festive meal.

I wonder how many times we have been like the prodigal son and how many times our Heavenly Father has extended grace when we deserved none.

 What detours have you chosen on your journey to Heaven that you need to ask for forgiveness today?

QUESTION TO CONSIDER: How can you live in such a way that people will not believe the talebearers?

To the prodigal son's surprise and delight, he was restored to the full privilege of being his father's son. He was transformed from a state of destitution to complete restoration. Not only are you forgiven of your sins, but you receive the spirit of sonship as His child, an heir of God and co-heir with Christ, of His incomparable riches.

Not until he's confronted with failure and despair,

does the prodigal son return home, repentant and willing to do anything to win back his father's favor. To his surprise, and the surprise of others, he's welcomed, without question, into his father's loving and forgiving arms.

> *He lifted me out of the pit of despair, out of the mud and the mire. He set my feet on solid ground and steadied me as I walked along. (Psalm 40:2, NLT)*

We have all sinned and deserve God's judgment. God, the Father, sent His only Son to satisfy that judgment for those who believe in Him. Jesus, the co-creator and eternal Son of God, who lived a sinless life, loves us so much that He died for our sins, taking the punishment that we deserve, was buried, and rose from the dead according to the Bible.

> *Who Himself bore our sins in His own body on the tree, that we, having died to sins, might live for righteousness—by whose stripes you were healed. (1 Peter 2:24)*

DAILY PRAYER: *As you pray, see yourself through the Father's eyes.*

Lord Jesus, I willingly submit my life to You today. I offer myself up as a living sacrifice, holy and pleasing to You. Forgive me for wrong judgments and give me the opportunity to walk in freedom. Forgive me for hurting those I love and assist me in becoming who You created me to be. Amen.

Prayer Reflections:

_____

_____

_____

_____

_____

_____

_____

_____

_____

_____

_____

_____

Day 13

There is No Surprise With God

 *Sometimes you create
your own storms!*

*Be still, and know that I am God; I will be
exalted among the nations, I will be exalted
in the earth! (Psalm 46:10)*

THOUGHT FOR TODAY: Many are called but few are chosen.

QUESTION TO CONSIDER: How can you allow God to heal you and move you forward?

When you allow God to heal you, you will then be able to move forward. *Joy is a decision, happiness is a choice.* It may not be okay today or tomorrow, but it's going to be okay. When you begin to call back the promises of God, you can then see the light at the end of the tunnel. Begin to help God - what you are putting in your spirit is what is coming out. Stop saying, "I wish," and start declaring life in your situation. You can be a water walker. You may not be the people's first choice but neither was David, the shepherd boy. David was being developed in the dark room of his life, out on the mountainside taking care of his father's sheep.

> *¹⁰ Thus Jesse made seven of his sons pass before Samuel. And Samuel said to Jesse, "The Lord has not chosen these." ¹¹ And Samuel said to Jesse, "Are all the young men here?" Then he said, "There remains yet the youngest, and there he is, keeping the sheep." And Samuel said to Jesse, "Send and bring him. For we will not sit down till he comes here." ¹² So he sent and brought him in. Now he was ruddy, with bright eyes, and good-looking. And the Lord said, "Arise, anoint him; for this is the one!" ¹³ Then Samuel took the horn of oil and anointed him in the midst of his brothers; and the Spirit of the Lord came upon David from that day forward. So Samuel arose and went to Ramah. (1 Samuel 16:10-13)*

Jesse had seven of his sons pass before Samuel, but Samuel said to him, "The Lord has not chosen these." He asked Jesse, "Are these all the sons you have?"

Jesse says, "There is still the youngest." *This is the first mention of David in the Bible and he was presented with no name.* You may feel unwanted or invisible as David felt and yet God had a plan for this young man. Samuel wanted the young man David to be brought before him. He would not sit until David was brought to him. Samuel immediately knew this young man was the one God had called out of obscurity to be anointed king! Samuel immediately anointed him in the presence of David's brothers and his father, and from that day, the Spirit of the Lord came powerfully upon David.

When the Lord anoints you into that place where He has called you, you then wonder why the doors aren't opening. You can be gifted, but it's nothing without the anointing.

You do not get the anointing without "the crushing".

You do not get the crushing without the process. The process for David happened thirteen years later when he eventually stepped into the position of king. He was anointed at 17 and appointed at 30 years of age. Those thirteen years were spent in the wilderness dodging spears and wrestling lions and bears. He was falsely accused and ran from Saul because of the jealousy Saul felt when he heard the women singing, "Saul has killed thousands but David tens of thousands." He lived in obscurity while God was preparing to develop him.

What obstacles have you had to face as you were being prepared for your anointing?

QUESTION TO CONSIDER: How can you speak life into your dying situation?

God takes you through the process of appointing to anointing. Even in your darkest times of life, God has a plan for your future. You must start by placing one foot in front of the other and moving forward. Just get out of bed today and allow God to move you along from one situation to the next until you step into His plan.

I have scrubbed floors and cleaned toilets while God was forging His way in me, so today I am blessed to be traveling the world for the Kingdom of God because I was faithful in the dark room of my life for six years. **He wanted to see how I would act without the cameras and stages.**

Could I handle popularity? To my humanness, I saw only a small bedroom at my parent's house, a low-income job and two sons that needed a fulltime mom. It looked like a dying situation to me, but to God, I was in the middle of a process.

Could David have ever dreamed that he would be king of Judah and Israel? This young man of 17 wasn't invited to his own party. It was an anointing party for the future king and David was the one left out.

However, God knew He had a plan.

You think God disqualifies you because of a divorce or an abortion, but God has a plan for you far beyond your mistakes.

DAILY PRAYER: *Search your heart and open your spiritual ears to hear what God has planned for you.*

Lord Jesus, I realize I do not deserve your goodness, however I know that You go far beyond my limitations and give me the strength to stand against all odds. I invite You to come into my life and change every situation that is not of You. Give me the fortitude to rise up while suggestion: remaining humble and honest with myself. Allow me to shed everything that is not like You and I decree I shall walk out the plan You have purposed for me. Amen.

Prayer Reflections:

_____

_____

_____

_____

_____

Day 14

From Pain to Purpose

 *Our mess becomes our message and our pain becomes our purpose.*

Keep your heart with all diligence, For out of it spring the issues of life. (Proverbs 4:23)

THOUGHT FOR TODAY: Detours are not always detours in God's plan.

QUESTION TO CONSIDER: How can you move pass your past?

There is pain in the process but peace in the promise. It will be worth it. Stop being distracted by certain people. Some people will hate you just because they see you getting the success they think they deserve from the work they haven't done. Haters are just confused fans.

Embrace the stormy seasons!

Sometimes it takes a storm for us to grow through pain in order for us to be blessed! Sunshine all the time makes a desert! Whatever path you have taken, God can and will use it for good if you will allow Him.

> *And Samuel said to Jesse, "Are all the young men here?" Then he said, "There remains yet the youngest, and there he is, keeping the sheep." And Samuel said to Jesse, "Send and bring him. For we will not sit down till he comes here." (1 Samuel 16:11)*

God is wanting to change your heart. If you bypass the wilderness journey, you are going to bypass open heart surgery. Stay focused and faithful where you are supposed to be.

God is going to where He assigned you, not where you assigned yourself.

When Samuel went to Jesse's house and was waiting for David to appear, he would not sit down. I'm sure Jesse, David's father, was worried about the prophet being uncomfortable. God will stop the whole party when it's time to bring you into your moment. Seven of Jesse's sons had passed before the prophet, but Samuel knew the chosen one had not appeared. God will find you when it's your time. *The process will not break you, it will make you.*

As king, David was a man of contrasts. He was single-mindedly committed to God, yet guilty of some of the most serious sins recorded in the Old Testament. David's life was a roller coaster of emotional highs and lows. He left us an example of passionate love of God and dozens of psalms, some of the most touching, beautiful poetry ever written.

His life was such a pattern of our lives today. David was courageous and strong in battle, trusting in God for protection, and he loved God deeply throughout his entire life; yet, he committed adultery with Bathsheba. He then tried to cover up her pregnancy, and when he failed with that, he had her husband Uriah the Hittite killed. And yet we see that God spoke about David in the book of Acts.

> *And when He had removed him (Saul), He raised up for them David as king, to whom also He gave testimony and said, 'I have found David the son of Jesse, a man after My own heart, who will do all My will.' (Acts 13:22)*

 List decisions in your life in which you need to forgive yourself to continue on your destiny.

QUESTION TO PONDER: How can you motivate yourself to go forward after failure?

But the Lord said to Samuel, "Do not look at his appearance or at his physical stature, because I have refused him. For the Lord does not see as man sees; for man looks at the outward appearance, but the Lord looks at the heart. (1 Samuel 16:7)

When Samuel was anointing David to become the future king, David was an innocent shepherd boy taking care of his father's sheep. He never dreamed he would sin against God because of the lust of a woman, Bathsheba.

To release your failures, know that God will accept your repentance and move you to your next season.

It's a heart issue. You can become cold-hearted in your sin and allow your carnal self to rule or move into true repentance as David did and allow God to direct the life steps He has already ordered for you.

23 The steps of a good man are ordered by the Lord, And He delights in his way. 24 Though he fall, he shall not be utterly cast down; For the Lord upholds him with His hand. (Psalm 37:23-24)

After repentance for his adulterous affair with Bathsheba, David walked through a dark season of the loss of their child. This is an example of your sins taking you further than you want to go and costing you more than you want to pay. The good news is God is waiting for you when you are ready to repent.

DAILY PRAYER: *Be honest with yourself and allow God to totally make you whole.*

Lord Jesus, I ask for forgiveness and release all the sins I have committed against You. I realize I live in a fallen world and will make other mistakes, but I know You are full of mercy and grace. When I come, You always respond. I give up today and allow You to be Lord of my life. Amen.

Prayer Reflections:

_____

_____

_____

_____

_____

_____

_____

_____

Day 15

Pursue your Passion

 *You will feel like a turtle stuck in peanut butter, not able to move forward.*

And do not be conformed to this world, but be transformed by the renewing of your mind, that you may prove what is that good and acceptable and perfect will of God. (Romans 12:2)

THOUGHT FOR TODAY: Life is a journey and the race is on.

QUESTION TO CONSIDER: How can I view my life experiences, the good, bad and bitter, through the lens of purpose?

So many times in life we want everyone supporting us before we'll step out of our comfort zone and do what's in our heart. Sometimes the people around you won't understand your journey, and they don't need to because it's not for them. God validates you, go forth! When God sees you doing your part, developing what He has given you, then He will jump in to do His part and open up doors no man can shut!

No matter how dark it looks, God never goes back on His word!

What God has for you, it is for YOU. What He has spoken over your life IS GOING to HAPPEN! The devil is a LIAR!! Whatever he is bringing against you to pull you down, will NOT prosper! When things get bitter and you feel you are on a detour, the question that you should not ask is, "Why am I going through this?" Instead ask, "Lord, how do you want to use this for my destiny?" If you can understand that God is working on preparing you for your destiny, you will be able to take on those challenges you are facing and know God is in the middle of it. So rejoice and praise Him.

When you buy into the world's value system, you will miss God's purpose for your life. Think about your values and where they are going to lead you. Do not wait for a major crisis or pain to come before you think about your life. Think 10 to 20 years from now and even into eternity. Look at Solomon's life.

> *I have seen all the works that are done under the sun; and indeed, all is vanity and grasping for the wind. (Ecclesiastes 1:14)*

Solomon had tried it all and yet he drifted from God's purpose in his life. *He realized without purpose, life is worthless.* The bottom line is, the world and its pleasures will pass away but those who do the will of God will live forever. There are certain aspects to God's purpose for you. The first is to be God's friend. God made you to know and love Him.

> *Jesus said to him, "'You shall love the Lord your God with all your heart, with all your soul, and with all your mind.' (Matthew 22:37)*

The second aspect to God's purpose is to do His will by helping others in life. What are you going to do with your God-given talents? The next aspect is to influence your world. What can you do to make life better for those in your life? The sooner you trust God in life, the longer you will benefit from His blessings. You often worry about missing the will of God for your life, but God works with your mistakes and bad decisions. His plans cannot be deterred. Just start moving.

What decisions can you make today that will change your tomorrow?

QUESTION TO PONDER: How can I eliminate those unimportant things to achieve my destiny?

Stop doing what isn't important so you can have time, money and energy to fulfill God's plan for you. To achieve your goals, you must understand your purpose. Take time out of your busy life to inspect your desires. Where do you spend your time? Everyone has 168 hours in a week. The difference between those who really make their lives count and those who don't is management. We all have the same amount of time, it's just the way you use it that counts. Where do you spend your money? Do you give God His first part?

> *⁹ Honor the Lord with your possessions, And with the first fruits of all your increase;*
> *¹⁰ So your barns will be filled with plenty, And your vats will overflow with new wine. (Proverbs 3:9-10)*

Everyone goes through trials in life and we know that life gets rough. We all have a void deep inside that only a relationship with Christ will fill. God made it so simple for us to accept His gift and salvation so that when times get tough, we know where to go. You were created with a specific design in mind; part of that purpose is a relationship with Jesus Christ. You were set apart before the beginning of the world

For *"whoever calls on the name of the Lord shall be saved." (Romans 10:13)*

DAILY PRAYER: *Ask Jesus Christ to reveal to you His purpose and give you the power to endure.*

Lord Jesus, I release all of my expectations and give you my heart. I realize I cannot accomplish Your plans for me without a true relationship with You. Help me to become the person You called me to be and give me the endurance to see Your plans come to pass. I yield myself to be the person You created me to be. Amen.

Prayer Reflections:

_____

_____

_____

_____

_____

_____

Day 16

Living in Your Purpose

 *God's possibilities meet your impossibility and life really becomes enjoyable.*

Yet in all these things we are more than conquerors through Him who loved us. (Romans 8:37)

THOUGHT FOR TODAY: Start today adjusting your life to the purposes of God.

QUESTION TO PONDER: How can I determine to make life changes and then walk those changes out in my life?

When you can realize that there are seasons in your life such as spring, summer, autumn and winter, you will be able to respond in a positive manner when going through the winter season.

Perseverance is the key to a breakthrough.

Too many of us stop short of what God has launched us towards. You give up right before it's time to go up and allow fear to paralyze you and stop your progress. You stop short of the purpose that has been promised to you by God. What you need is the mindset to persevere until you see the promises of God manifesting in your life.

> *For all the promises of God in Him are Yes, and in Him Amen, to the glory of God through us. (2 Corinthians 1:20)*

God's plans go far beyond time and into eternity. No matter how difficult the journey, you have to make up your mind and heart that you will not give in or give up. The word *"persevere"* means to persist in anything undertaken; maintain a purpose in spite of difficulty, obstacles or discouragement, and continue steadfastly. Make sure you are investing your life, time and resources in things that are lasting and not things that will pass away. There is a story in Joshua 6 that explains that God had promised the land beyond the Jordan River to His people, but they had not taken possession of it.

> *¹ Now Jericho was securely shut up because of the children of Israel; none went out, and*

none came in. ² And the Lord said to Joshua: "See! I have given Jericho into your hand, its king, and the mighty men of valor. ³ You shall march around the city, all you men of war; you shall go all around the city once. This you shall do six days. 4 And seven priests shall bear seven trumpets of rams' horns before the ark. But the seventh day you shall march around the city seven times, and the priests shall blow the trumpets. ⁵ It shall come to pass, when they make a long blast with the ram's horn, and when you hear the sound of the trumpet, that all the people shall shout with a great shout; then the wall of the city will fall down flat. And the people shall go up every man straight before him." (Joshua 6:1-5)

The children of Israel were about to possess the land that God had promised to Abraham, Isaac, Jacob and Moses, but they had to march. Think about the inner battle of fear these people were facing. This was the first city to be conquered. *Your first battle is always your hardest.* Just getting up and doing it is half the battle. Joshua spent forty-five years in the wilderness getting ready for the battle of Jericho.

What battles are you facing that are keeping you from your purpose?

QUESTION TO PONDER: How can I know that, without a doubt, greater is He that is in me?

Look at the circumstances facing Joshua and the children of Israel. Jericho was a small city and should have taken only about one hour to walk around the walls. The problem was the walls were so high and wide. Our problem is that our perspective gets clouded by how high and wide the walls are to get to the promises that God has given us.

There are thousands of promises in the Bible for God's people.

This is why worship becomes so important to us. It lifts our perspective so that we can see over the walls or over our obstacles and opposition. You see, God makes promises to many of us that we never possess because we refuse to persevere. If you don't recognize that God created you for eternity, you will invest in the wrong direction and believe what people say.

Blessed be the God and Father of our Lord Jesus Christ, who has blessed us with every spiritual blessing in the heavenly places in Christ. (Ephesians 1:3)

Everything that is in Jesus Christ should be operating in your life: His strength, love, joy, peace and power. However, you must fight the fight of faith to possess it and live in it. *The war is in your mind (soul).* However, when you worship your great God, it will elevate your perspective and help you to begin to believe that nothing is too hard for Him.

DAILY PRAYER: *Allow God to increase your faith as you direct your thoughts toward Him.*

Lord Jesus, I realize I live in a fallen world of negativity. For me to accomplish the greatness that you have called me to do, I totally rely on You and Your promises. Today, I decree that I will finish my race and excel on the course of life that You have purposed for me. Amen.

Prayer Reflections:

_____

_____

_____

_____

_____

_____

Day 17

Get Up, Get Out

Miracles are easy to get but hard to keep.

¹ I will bless the Lord at all times; His praise shall continually be in my mouth. ² My soul shall make its boast in the Lord; The humble shall hear of it and be glad. ³ Oh, magnify the Lord with me, And let us exalt His name together. (Psalms 34:1-3)

THOUGHT FOR TODAY: For there to be a miracle, there must first be a problem.

QUESTION TO CONSIDER: Why is the path to a miracle always through uncomfortable territory?

Jesus isn't revealed in your easy, He is revealed in your storm. You will begin to see that the enemy you are intimidated by is also intimated by you. In Joshua 6, we see that the children of Israel were facing the walled city of Jericho. They needed a miracle.

> *¹ Now Jericho was securely shut up because of the children of Israel; none went out, and none came in. ² And the Lord said to Joshua: "See! I have given Jericho into your hand, its king, and the mighty men of valor. (Joshua 6:1-2)*

Jericho was securely shut up because of the children of Israel; none went out and none came in. Yet the Lord tells Joshua that He has given Jericho into his hand. *These verses do not go together.* The problem with verse two is verse one. Only God can speak in past tense about a battle you haven't even fought yet. That is how confident God is that He does that for you. He gives you promises and just expects you to walk out those promises. God says that I've already given you your answer. Just take it.

Have you ever felt like what you see in your life doesn't match up with what God has said in your heart? All Joshua could see were the walls surrounding Jericho, however he believed God. He could not even see the enemy who was protected inside, and yet he trusted God. Has God ever asked you to do something so out of your comfort zone that you "knew" it could not be God? Sometimes we think we know more than we actually know! Friend, that is the God I serve. God wants you to trust Him all the way. *Sometimes our revelation does not match our reality.* At this time in your life is when you need people to help you see over your walls or obstacles.

Joshua gave instructions to the priests and the people as they began their first day of takeover. The miracle did not happen on the first day nor the second. *It took seven days before the wall came down, however the wall did come down.* Our progress in our challenges are not always obvious. Can you imagine how the army of Israel felt as they began marching? They thought they were going into battle. *Instead they began taking a walk around a city,* not one day but for seven days. How many times have you questioned God because your answer did not come quick enough? I would think, if I was God, I would have shown the Israelites some progress during those seven days just to keep them motivated. Then they were not allowed to talk about it. Joshua knew that their mouths and thoughts could stop the promises of God, which is why he had the people remain silent.

 What problems in your life need to be conquered to consummate a miracle?

QUESTION TO PONDER: How can I allow God's process to be completed in me?

As people living in a fallen world, we must see progress or we lose attention quickly. Joshua had only told the children of Israel to march. He did not give them specific instructions as to time or process.

> *15 But it came to pass on the seventh day that they rose early, about the dawning of the day, and marched around the city seven times in the same manner. On that day only they marched around the city seven times. 16 And the seventh time it happened, when the priests blew the trumpets, that Joshua said to the people: "Shout, for the Lord has given you the city! 20 So the people shouted when the priests blew the trumpets. And it happened when the people heard the sound of the trumpet, and the people shouted with a great shout, that the wall fell down flat. Then the people went up into the city, every man straight before him, and they took the city. (Joshua 6:15-16, 20)*

The process is indefinite.

If a portion of the walls of Jericho had fallen each day, the children of Israel would not have needed to trust God with the end result. God wants to know you will trust Him all the way. It was while the Israelites were walking around the walls that God was preparing them to fight the giants in the land. *It is while living for God daily that He is preparing us for greater things ahead.* Remember God is more concerned with your character than your comfort. He cares more about what He is doing inside you than what you are doing on the outside.

DAILY PRAYER: *Submit your dreams to God so He can show you miracles in your future.*

Lord Jesus, I offer myself up as a vessel to be used by You to develop my character. I cannot see my future, however I believe You will direct my path while You prepare me for greater things ahead. Amen.

Prayer Reflections:

_____

_____

_____

_____

_____

_____

_____

Day 18

Never Go Back

*Get up and help God help you!
Don't let time make you doubt what
God told you would happen.*

*Keep your heart with all diligence, For out
of it spring the issues of life. (Proverbs 4:23)*

*^{37} Jesus said to him, "'You shall love the
Lord your God with all your heart, with
all your soul, and with all your mind.' ^{38}
This is the first and great commandment.
^{39} And the second is like it: 'You shall love
your neighbor as yourself.' ^{40} On these two
commandments hang all the Law and the
Prophets." (Matthew 22:37-40)*

THOUGHT FOR TODAY: Don't fear it when you can
faith it.

QUESTION TO CONSIDER: How can I praise God on credit until my change happens?

Fear is a magnet to the very thing you don't want. You either stand in faith or fear. We know that where the spirit of the Lord is, there is freedom and as long as you pray, you will not stray. Many times your circumstances do not change; however, you can still walk in peace. Matthew tells us to love others as we love ourselves. That can be the root of the problem because many times, we do not love ourselves. We love God with our broken hearts, broken souls and broken minds. It's not ironic that the Lord Jesus starts with your heart. Why? Because the heart is where the passion originates, and without passion, nothing matters. How is your passion for Jesus? If your heart is not in it, it will become a boring obligation.

When your heart is toxic, you are then headed for a spiritual heart attack. You then need spiritual open-heart surgery to get your joy back. When you are passionate about your journey with the Lord Jesus, you are never forced to serve Him.

> *For out of the heart proceed evil thoughts,*
> *murders, adulteries, fornications, thefts,*
> *false witness, blasphemies. (Matthew 15:19)*

Christianity works from the inside out, not the outside in. We are spirit, soul and body. Just because my spirit is born again doesn't mean my body is also, and just because we accept Jesus Christ as Lord doesn't mean it creates a healthy physical body. In order to expect a healthy body, I still need to exercise and eat nutritious foods. Just because you accepted Jesus Christ one day doesn't mean your broken heart is healed immediately.

Your soul is wounded.

Many times you try to medicate or apply superficial healing with drugs or illicit sex. The Spirit of God must come in and put His light in those dark places of your soul. You have vowed that no one will ever hurt you again so you padlock your heart for protection. You visit God on Sundays and Wednesdays while putting a Band-Aid on those broken areas. My prayer is that you stop just visiting God and allow Him to invade your inner most being.

 What areas of your spirit, soul and body are you needing to release and allow God to work through you?

QUESTION TO CONSIDER: How can I walk in forgiveness daily?

Forgiveness is full of compassion but it demands a change in conduct. Jesus is our example of total forgiveness and never going back. To forgive without demanding a change of conduct is to make the grace of God an accomplice to evil. You cannot say I forgive without acting on it in the compassion of Jesus Christ.

Forgiving those who have wounded you frees you to face tomorrow without carrying baggage of the past. Unforgiveness is actually taking something that belongs to God, and taking matters into your own hands.

> *Beloved, do not avenge yourselves, but rather give place to wrath; for it is written, "Vengeance is Mine, I will repay," says the Lord. (Romans 12:19)*

Make what Jesus did for you greater than what others have done to you. Jesus said that vengeance belongs to Him. It is not your responsibility to bring retribution on those who have wounded you. When you allow unforgiveness to remain, you then are allowing pitiful thoughts to hold you hostage. The devil loves to put negative thoughts in your mind, but it doesn't mean you have to ride that train of thinking on the track of unforgiveness.

Paul instructed us in Philippians 4:8 to meditate only on those things which are virtuous and praiseworthy. Through experience, Paul knew how to live above his challenges. It had to be accomplished through the power of the Holy Spirit. Paul let us know that we can do all things through Christ who strengthens us.

DAILY PRAYER: *Meditate on the Word of the Lord as you pray.*

Lord Jesus, Your word says that I can do all things through Christ who strengthens me. I ask today that You enlighten me to those challenges that have kept me hostage, and give me the strength to let them go. I forgive those who have wronged me and release the pain that has crippled me. I am free today in Jesus' name! Amen.

Prayer Reflections:

_____

_____

_____

_____

_____

_____

_____

_____

_____

_____

Day 19

Trust God

 *As long as you pray,*
you will not stray.

But if we hope for what we do not see,
we eagerly wait for it with perseverance.
(Romans 8:25)

THOUGHT FOR TODAY: Trust God even when you cannot trace Him!

QUESTION TO CONSIDER: Can you trust God when you are faced with adverse situations and circumstances?

What do you do when you are facing tragedy and life's various challenges? *Trust God.* That is a simple two-word response until you find yourself living the tragedy or faced with a challenge. It is very easy to trust God when life is good but what about when your world is being turned upside down. How then do we trust God?

By faith Abraham obeyed when he was called to go out to the place which he would receive as an inheritance. And he went out, not knowing where he was going. (Hebrews 11:8)

The story of Abraham and Sarah in the book of Genesis began in the city of Ur, a busy city near the coastline of the Persian Gulf. He was the man repulsed by the idolatry and sin of Ur because he had come to know the one true and living God. In fact, God had instructed Abraham to leave his country and go to the land that He would show him. God gave Abraham a promise that He would make him a great nation. That He would bless everyone who blessed Abraham and curse those who cursed him. Armed with only a promise, Abraham, along with his father, his nephew Lot, and wife, Sarah, began the journey of their life. This journey was all about trust.

> *Is anything too hard for the Lord? At the appointed time I will return to you, according to the time of life, and Sarah shall have a son." (Genesis 18:14)*

Besides traveling from place to place for years, Abraham and Sarah never had a child. God then gave them a promise that they would give birth to a son despite being well beyond the child-bearing age. Sarah laughed when she heard that she, a woman in her nineties, was going to give birth.

The Lord then asked Abraham, "Is anything too hard for me?"

Sarah was an intelligent and capable woman who established her mission in life to help her husband fulfill God's purposes. That was not a weakness.

Trusting God requires strength.

Some wives have systematically sabotaged God's plan for their husbands because they have not been willing to believe God and entrust themselves to His wisdom. They simply will not trust God to work through their husbands to accomplish God's will in their lives.

What areas of your life have you needed to allow God to take His place as Lord?

QUESTION TO CONSIDER: How can you know God's will for your life?

Sarah saw her faith tested and her submissiveness sorely tried many times as she traveled with Abraham. Faith grows best under attack. The person who prays for God to remove all problems may be asking for a sickly spiritual life. Sometimes your faith may falter under stress, but if you admit your failure and accept God's forgiveness, even your failures can contribute to your spiritual growth.

In Hebrews 11, Abraham and Sarah are commended for their great faith, but their failures are recorded for our instruction and encouragement. More than once they were able to humbly go back to God and seek His will. Did they fail? To know God's will for your life means you must walk in faith, not knowing what tomorrow will bring, but definitely know who holds tomorrow.

Even great men and women of God have their moments of faithlessness. The life of faith is never free from challenges. Sarah was one of those women whom King Lemuel spoke about, who did her husband good and not evil all the days of her life in Proverbs 31. A woman can only be that kind of wife when she believes that nothing is too difficult for God, and when she truly believes that God can even use her husband's mistakes to bring Him glory and blessings to their lives.

Sarah did indeed have a son, and his name was Isaac. Isaac became a patriarch of the Jewish nation and made his parents proud. Can you trust that God has your best interest at heart? Can you believe God even when you feel like a failure? Abraham got up more times than he fell down. He made a choice and so can you!

DAILY PRAYER: *Allow the Lord to shine His searchlight on you as you seek Him today.*

Lord Jesus, today I release my desires, my frustrations and my fears to You. I want to know You for who You truly are, my Father who created me for greatness. Help me to allow my failures to cause me to become stronger in the spirit and grow daily in faith. Amen.

Prayer Reflections:

_____

_____

_____

_____

_____

_____

_____

_____

_____

_____

_____

Day 20

Faith over Fear

 *Fear is the enemy to faith, therefore it is my enemy too!*

"Do not be afraid of them. Remember the Lord is great and awesome... God will fight for us" (Nehemiah 4:14, 19).

THOUGHT FOR TODAY: God is faithful even when I am not!

QUESTION TO CONSIDER: In what areas of your life have you failed to surrender your will because of fear?

Faith in God is an attribute every believer possesses. According to Hebrews 11:6, when we approach God we must do so in total belief of who He is. Fear and faith are complete opposites. You cannot have faith in God while yet walking in fear. If you are living in fear, you have no faith in God.

> *But without faith it is impossible to please him: for he that cometh to God must believe that he is, and that he is a rewarder of them that diligently seek him. (Hebrews 11:6)*

Remember the day in Mark 5 when Jesus was on His way to heal Jairus's daughter? A large crowd followed and pressed around Him. A woman was in the crowd who had been bleeding for twelve years and had suffered a great deal under the care of many doctors. She had spent her life's earning, yet she was getting worse. When she heard about Jesus, she went up behind him in the crowd and touched his robe because she thought that, if she could just touch his clothes, she would be made whole. Immediately her bleeding stopped and she felt in her body that she was freed from her suffering.

> *30 And Jesus, immediately knowing in Himself that power had gone out of Him, turned around in the crowd and said, "Who touched My clothes?" 31 But His disciples said to Him, "You see the multitude thronging You, and You say, 'Who touched Me?'" (Mark 5:30-31)*

Jesus wanted to know who had caused the anointed

healing to leave His body but there were too many people in the crowd. The disciples had no idea who could have been that one that touched Jesus to make Him stop and take notice. As Jesus was looking through the crowd, the woman, knowing what had happened to her, fell at His feet and, trembling with fear, told Him the whole truth. Jesus said to her, "Daughter, your faith has healed you. Go in peace and be healed from your suffering." This woman will always be known as the woman with the issue of blood; however, everyone knows her as a woman who faced her fear and touched Jesus anyway.

To receive God's commendation in the middle of an impossible situation, you must exercise your faith. You just face your fear and do it anyway.

Life without faith is a life with fear.

If you do not have faith in God, you live by your own power and strength. While this might carry someone for a while, in the end it is not enough. Knowledge about God and faith in God are not the same. Often something happens in our life to act as that faith catalyst to point us to Jesus Christ. The woman with the issue of blood had been everywhere looking for an answer for twelve long years. No one could help her. But God! When she heard that Jesus was in town, she was afraid that, once again, she would be disappointed.

Yet she fought through the crowd to touch His garment. That's all it took for her.

What fears have you harbored that have kept you imprisoned?

QUESTION TO CONSIDER: Can fear and faith exist together?

Faith is the absolute belief that God is constantly working behind the scenes in every area of your life, even when there is no evidence to support this fact. As faith and belief gains the upper hand in our thoughts, fear takes hold of our emotions while trying to rule us. Our deliverance from fear and even worry is based on our faith.

So then faith comes by hearing, and hearing by the word of God. (Romans 10:17)

It is through the consistent study of God's word, prayer and meditation that we begin to experience a strong, confident faith that excludes worry and fear. The woman with the issue of blood was tormented for twelve years. The average person would have given up hope and would never have fought their way through a crowd to touch Jesus. As fear was trying to control her emotions, she reached deep inside her being and put faith into action.

The safest place is right smack dab in the middle of God's will.

He wants what is best for your life. One of the happiest and most peaceful moments ever is when you decide to let go of what you cannot change and truly trust God!

Trusting God even though all hell might be breaking loose around you is called victory. You do your part and let God do His! He specializes in your impossibilities! Remember, you are a victor, not just a survivor.

DAILY PRAYER: *Release your faith as you give Jesus your cares.*

Lord Jesus, even though I walk through the valley of fear in my life, I refuse to allow it to rule me. I release all fear and worry and decree and declare that I walk by faith and not by sight. I will allow You to direct my steps and lead me into paths of righteousness daily. I am a water walker and shall do the will of the Father in my life. Amen.

Prayer Reflections:

_____

_____

Day 21

Sometimes Life Just Happens

 Ships don't sink because of the water around them, ships sink because of the water that gets IN them.

[22] that you put off, concerning your former conduct, the old man which grows corrupt according to the deceitful lusts, [23] and be renewed in the spirit of your mind, [24] and that you put on the new man which was created according to God, in true righteousness and holiness. (Ephesians 4:22-24)

THOUGHT FOR TODAY: Don't let what is happening around you get inside and weigh you down.

QUESTION TO CONSIDER: Are you being squeezed by the world or being shaped by God?

As you squeeze a toothpaste tube, that tube begins

to lose its shape and will eventually end up flat with no toothpaste inside. What was inside has been used up. However, when you buy a bag of balloons, you see empty balloons with no shape at all. As you breathe into a balloon it takes on a new life or shape and it will keep that shape until the air is released. *This illustrates the importance of outside influences in our lives.* In Matthew 5, Jesus tells us that we are to be salt and light in our world to those we influence daily. We realize salt is hidden but light is obvious. Jesus was telling us that He wants us to be influencers for His glory because salt and light have the ability to alter their world.

> *13 "You are the salt of the earth; but if the salt loses its flavor, how shall it be seasoned? It is then good for nothing but to be thrown out and trampled underfoot by men. 14 "You are the light of the world. A city that is set on a hill cannot be hidden. 15 Nor do they light a lamp and put it under a basket, but on a lamp stand, and it gives light to all who are in the house. 16 Let your light so shine before men, that they may see your good works and glorify your Father in heaven. (Matthew 5:14-15)*

Be careful who you put on your team. You cannot be salt and light when those around you do not see the presence of the Holy Spirit within you. Learn to get to know those who labor among you. Slow down on allowing people to get too close too quickly and watch people's fruit. I've spent so much of my life trusting people too much and putting them into positions they were not ready to assume while not inspecting their fruit. Allowing folks to talk about others in front of me without realizing if they talk about others with me, they are doing the same about me to others.

I want you to grow today.

You outgrow people just like you outgrow clothes. Some people cannot go where God is taking you because they cannot handle it. Even though it hurts at times, we must realize that God sees the beginning to the end. He's not hurting you by removing certain people. Do not make chapters for those only meant for a sentence in your life.

Keep the faith. The most amazing things in life tend to happen right at the moment you're about to give up hope. Loyalty means I'm down with you whether you are wrong or right. But I will tell you when you're wrong and help you get it right. God knew you were capable of great things in life so He called you where you are today! Now give Him a chance to come through for you. Be that salt and light that is needed for those friends who are hurting.

 *List examples of being salt and
light to your friends today.*

QUESTION TO CONSIDER: How can you make positive decisions today that will alter your friends' lives for the good?

Everyone experiences loneliness and times of feeling insecure and even rejection. I have found it is during these times, that you run, not walk, to the foot of the cross and look for Him. Be patient when that trial comes. Sometimes you lose your focus about God's plan when He has already worked out the plan. It's just up to you to get back into His presence and allow Him to complete a good work in you. When you allow Him to work through you, you will then see changes.

> *²³ The steps of a good man are ordered by the Lord, And He delights in his way. ²⁴ Though he fall, he shall not be utterly cast down; For the Lord upholds him with His hand all around you because you influence those friends in your life. (Psalms 37:23-24)*

You do not seek God just for God because each of us are influencers. There are people watching you to see how you will deal with life today. They need to see stability, wholeness, peace, joy, love and contentment.

Where will they find it? In you, my friend.

God has a plan for you to change those lives who are in your world but it's up to you to allow God to be Lord of every decision you make. So do not hate those stormy seasons when you cannot do anything but fall at Jesus' feet. It is during these times that you will become whole in Him and as you become whole, you will be that salt and light that those in your life are needing.

DAILY PRAYER: *Allow God to mold you into that influencer who will change your world.*

Lord Jesus, today I pray divine connections and favor in my life. I will discern the gifts of God and receive them with an open heart. I command all hidden, evil motives and wrongdoings by those who surround me to be exposed. I pray that those that I am to influence in my life will bring fulfillment and purpose to me. Amen.

Prayer Reflections:

Day 22

Hit Pause and Trust the Process

 The enemy will attempt to paralyze us from praying and seeking God for these painful situations in our lives.

Why are you cast down, O my soul? And why are you disquieted within me? Hope in God; For I shall yet praise Him, The help of my countenance and my God. (Psalm 42:11)

THOUGHT FOR TODAY: There are seasons in your life when you must pause.

QUESTION TO CONSIDER: How can you walk in faith when you feel overwhelmed?

In life you will go through moments that you must hit pause and trust the process that God has for you until the end. Because you are in a delay process for an answer from God does not mean He has denied your request. Remember that He who began a good work in you is faithful to finish it. Throughout the book of Psalms, David would insert a word or phrase at times to evoke an emotion that would create a reflection. You then realize that there will be seasons in your life where you must pause and reflect back on the hand of God in your life.

I can honestly say that reflecting back through my life has given me more faith to obediently proceed throughout, not only this day, but also tomorrow. There will be times when you will feel overwhelmed, however even David lets us know there is hope in God.

> *David therefore departed from there and escaped to the cave of Adullam. So when his brothers and all his father's house heard it, they went down there to him.2 And everyone who was in distress, everyone who was in debt, and everyone who was discontented gathered to him. So he became captain over them. And there were about four hundred men with him. (1 Samuel 22:1-2)*

King David felt overwhelmed and alone. This is true no matter who you are or what status in life you may have achieved, the thing you must remember is that no matter what others are saying, what you are facing is real to you, and David was no different than we are. He was overlooked by his own father, and all the while, God recognized him as king. He served King Saul who did not respect him, fought Goliath while on an errand to carry food to his brothers, and found himself from the pasture to the palace within twenty-four hours. Even though David was loyal to Saul, Saul became obsessed with the death of David. So David runs and has to leave his wife, his job, his family, and friends to hide in a cave.

Life can change your circumstances in one minute if you do not know who you are in Christ.

David ended up hiding in a cave. He just wanted to get away, however he wrote two psalms while in this cave.

> *¹ I cry out to the Lord with my voice; With my voice to the Lord I make my supplication. ² I pour out my complaint before Him; I declare before Him my trouble. (Psalm 142:1-2)*

> *Be merciful to me, O God, be merciful to me! For my soul trusts in You; And in the shadow of Your wings I will make my refuge, Until these calamities have passed by. (Psalm 57:1)*

Consider situations in your life that cause you to want to run away.

Question to Consider: Even when overwhelmed, how can you stand strong in the reality that God is in control?

Maybe you are there today, overwhelmed, feeling hopeless, in the cave, or maybe you feel the pressure of fear that God is no longer with you. Even the most spiritually mature and strong can become overwhelmed at times. Remember that in the most overwhelming time of his life, Jesus Christ sweated great drops of blood.

> ²⁹ *He gives power to the weak, And to those who have no might He increases strength.* ³⁰ *Even the youths shall faint and be weary, And the young men shall utterly fall,* ³¹ *But those who wait on the Lord shall renew their strength; They shall mount up with wings like eagles, They shall run and not be weary, They shall walk and not faint.* (Isaiah 40:29-31)

You may feel overwhelmed; however, God is over all. You may feel low, but God is Creator of the entire universe and holds you in the palm of His hand. So, what do you do when you feel like the world is on top of you? You magnify the Lord, focus on Him and enlarge Him.

> *For the eyes of the* LORD *run to and fro throughout the whole earth, to show Himself strong on behalf of those whose heart is loyal to Him... (2 Chronicles 16:9)*

DAILY PRAYER: *Allow God to be your focus as you pray.*

Lord Jesus, nothing in all creation is hidden from You. You have given me weapons that are not carnal but mighty for pulling down strongholds! I will not allow life's challenges to overwhelm me. I understand that just because my answer is delayed, it is not denied. Lord, I know you realize what is best for me. I stand on your promise! Amen.

Prayer Reflections:

_____

_____

_____

Day 23

Delays Aren't Denials

Living by faith is not living by feelings.

² And the Lord was with Joseph, and he was a prosperous man; and he was in the house of his master the Egyptian ³ And his master saw that the Lord was with him, and that the Lord made all that he did to prosper in his hand. ⁴ And Joseph found grace in his sight, and he served him: and he made him overseer over his house, and all that he had he put into his hand. (Genesis 39:2-4)

THOUGHT FOR TODAY: God's favor is in every believer's life through Jesus.

QUESTION TO CONSIDER: Does God allow trials and tests in a believer's life?

You cannot be good enough to earn God's favor and yet God's favor is in every believer's life through Jesus Christ. In Psalm 5:12, David was speaking to God when he stated that the Lord will bless the righteous and with favor He will surround him as a shield. In his captivity, God was surrounding Joseph with a shield of favor on every level. Potiphar, Joseph's master, saw the blessings of God on Joseph and gave him advancements in his house. It did not happen immediately, however Joseph remained loyal in his service to Potiphar. As surely as God has promised that He made us kings and priests to reign in life, He also allows times and seasons of testing and perfecting. You must be able to discern the difference between delays and denials or you will lose your peace and stop pursuing your purpose.

In 1 Samuel 30:1-8, David gives us an example of losing everything and yet not losing hope. David and his men had returned to Ziklag, their home, after a battle and found everything burned and their families kidnapped. For a short time, this entire group of men wept until they could weep no more. They had lost the most precious possessions in their lives. Living by faith is not living without feelings. It is alright to weep because joy is going to come in the morning. We need to pass through the valley of tears but not build a house there. David overhears that all the people were talking about stoning him because everyone was overcome with grief. Here is the most powerful statement that will set you free in time of delay and denial. First Samuel 30:6 says that David strengthened himself in the Lord!!

> *Now David was greatly distressed, for the people spoke of stoning him, because the soul of all the people was grieved, every man for his sons and his daughters. But David strengthened himself in the Lord his God. (1 Samuel 30:6)*

David had lost his family, and now those closest to him were turning against him. His day went from bad to worse. Don't get bitter, get better. Bitterness begins as a seed of offense and turns into a root that affects your fruit in life. You must choose to forgive. Opportunities to get bitter are always going to be there, however you must choose to not live there. You must praise your way through the wilderness as David did. He did not have false hope and ignored the problems. His family was gone, however he simply magnified the Lord his God above his problems. Don't talk to God about how big your problems are, talk to your problems about how big your God is.

 How can you change your perspective to change your life?

Question to Consider: What do you do during the delay seasons in your life?

We see examples in God's word that helps keep us focused when we lose our way. Look at David and use his life as a road map to guide you along when you feel utterly hopeless and helpless. David was just a normal man who faced challenges just like you and me, and yet he rose above his storms. David dressed himself in the ephod and began worshipping God while he inquired of the Lord.

Lord, what do I do in this hopeless situation?

I feel like a failure and yet I am still living each day. David had focused faith during his delay season and did not ask God if he should stay and wait for an answer. Instead he asked if he should get up and go. God's directive will always get you moving from your seat of comfort, and He will always require you to participate in your recovery program. Faith requires action.

> *And raised us up together, and made us sit together in the heavenly places in Christ Jesus. (Ephesians 2:6)*

Remind yourself where you are seated. Change your vision from defeat to victory. From loss to recovery.

God wants you to live a life of victory, not defeat. Remember that life is a marathon, not just a sprint. Just because you are facing delay does not mean you will always live there. Desire will give you the drive to do something about your situation. Fight from a position of victory, not for a position of victory.

DAILY PRAYER: *Position yourself in prayer and prepare for total recovery.*

Lord Jesus, I know that all things work together for good to those who love the Lord and that are called according to His purpose. I stand in faith believing that this storm will pass. Allow me to be an agent of Your grace in the lives of others while helping them recover all. Amen.

Prayer Reflections:

_____

_____

_____

_____

_____

_____

_____

Day 24

Relax, Let Go and Let God

 Anointing will get you to your purpose but character keeps you there.

¹ And Ahab told Jezebel all that Elijah had done, also how he had executed all the prophets with the sword. ² Then Jezebel sent a messenger to Elijah, saying, "So let the gods do to me, and more also, if I do not make your life as the life of one of them by tomorrow about this time." ³ And when he saw that, he arose and ran for his life, and went to Beersheba, which belongs to Judah, and left his servant there. (1 Kings 19:1-3)

THOUGHT FOR TODAY: Do not make decisions in moments of anxiety or high stress.

QUESTION TO CONSIDER: Can God take you past your last act of obedience?

Elijah the prophet was a lover and follower of God and yet he had a moment in his life that created great anxiety. Elijah was a man of character dealing with Ahab and Jezebel whose true purpose was to destroy Elijah. Many times, your greatest tests come immediately after a victory. Elijah had defeated 850 false prophets and commanded the rain to fall after three-and-a-half years of drought, which he had prophesied. Out of this season of victory comes Elijah's greatest test of faith. It is true in your life as well. When you experience a triumph, the enemy will try to create a tidal wave of anxiety, fear and paralyzing dread for the future. Elijah who was full of character and faith, began running for his life. God confronted him, "Elijah, what are you doing?" Stress and anxiety will cause you to miss God or delay obedience to God's instructions. You may not slay 450 prophets of Baal and 450 prophets of Asherah as Elijah did, however you are a giant slayer in every right.

> And he said, "I have been very zealous for the Lord God of hosts; because the children of Israel have forsaken Your covenant, torn down Your altars, and killed Your prophets with the sword. I alone am left; and they seek to take my life." (1 Kings 19:14)

Yet I have reserved seven thousand in Israel,
all whose knees have not bowed to Baal,
and every mouth that has not kissed him."
(1 Kings 19:18)

It was so easy for Elijah to forget what God had done for him as he ran for his life. Just one threat from Jezebel, and Elijah is ruled by his current problem. At times, you too can allow doctor's diagnosis, pink slips from your company, divorce papers or even someone getting the promotion you earned, steal your focus. I've witnessed and experienced these situations in my life. Doing everything that I knew to do and allowing the stress of one moment to paralyze me and force me into depression.

Sometimes even your own bad decisions can cause you to get into a place of anxiety. Elijah truly believed he was the last prophet standing. God had to remind him that he still had 7,000 in Israel that had not bowed to Baal. In your eyes, you see brokenness, rejection, hopelessness, but in God's eyes, He sees a warrior, a victor, and strength!

 Name a situation in your life that you need to see God restore.

QUESTION TO CONSIDER: How can you overcome the fear of others' opinions?

You can get anxious about what others are saying at church, on social media, and even in your family. There will be times when you know you are doing your best to honor God and people will begin judging and talking. You must not spend your energy fearing what your critics say. Instead begin praying and watch God turn everything around. There are no sudden lies in God. He is never surprised by our life challenges. Who gives your critics permission to speak into your life? The people who matter don't judge us, and the people who judge us don't matter. Forgetting what God did, Elijah begins fearing Jezebel and runs for his life into isolation.

When you allow your challenges to rule you, you will ignore your next assignment in life.

Even though he was a normal man full of fear of the unknown, God did not stop using Elijah until He called him to Heaven.

There are times in life when God has given you directions and, because of anxiety or fear, you miss your next assignment. Recharge your spirit and body, renew your worship and refocus your life.

Do not allow the noise of life to drown out the voice of God.

God instructed Elijah to select his successor, the

man Elisha, and he lived eighteen years serving God, performing miracles and raising up that next generation leader. Today get your eyes off your problem and on your purpose. I challenge you to be like Jesus to someone you meet today.

DAILY PRAYER: *Release those problems that have you traumatized.*

Lord Jesus, teach me to not let my heart be troubled. Because You live, I also live in You through the Holy Spirit. I thank You that Your word assures me that there is now no condemnation for me because I am in Christ Jesus. I rejoice in Your promise that You will go before me and make the rough places smooth. Amen.

Prayer Reflections:

_____

_____

_____

_____

_____

_____

Day 25

God is Still Over All

God is the God of the comeback.

Fear not, for I am with you; Be not dismayed, for I am your God. I will strengthen you, Yes, I will help you, I will uphold you with My righteous right hand.' (Isaiah 41:10)

THOUGHT FOR TODAY: Once fear creeps in, doubt isn't far behind.

QUESTION TO CONSIDER: How does Jesus give you a do over?

God specifically speaks to fear in your life because He knows you will have plenty of opportunities to fear. There has never been another century in history as today. You can see wars, murders, Ebola, economic crashes, ISIS in real time on television. Three of four Americans say they feel more fearful today than they did twenty years ago. Loss of job, loss of marriage, drug addictions are just a few of the fears that people face daily. What do we know about fear? We know it is contagious, limiting and draining. Once you open the door to fear, doubt is the next to come. God understood you would fear when He said, "Fear not."

Remember that God is faithful not because we are good but because His nature is to be faithful. The enemy will tell you lies such as 'you deserve brokenness,' 'this punishment is for something you allowed in your past', but the truth is that Jesus declared it finished in John 19. He was declaring that all of our sins and failures were taken care of by His act of humility on Calvary. This one act is how Jesus gives you a do over - new mercy, new grace, and even a new life.

> *So when Jesus had received the sour wine, He said, "It is finished!" And bowing His head, He gave up His spirit. (John 19:30)*

Doubt will cause you to neglect faith and embrace fear. The acronym for fear is "false evidence appearing real." Fear can come in an instant and throw your life into a chaotic situation. The immediate effect of fear is to shut you down and you cannot seem to move forward. God says that if that situation in your life is not good, then He's not done with you.

And we know that all things work together for good to those who love God, to those who are the called according to His purpose. (Romans 8:28)

What do you do when you are overwhelmed by doubt and it brings on fear? When you are served with divorce papers or you realize your child is addicted to drugs. Remember if your life is not good, God is not finished with you. In John 11, Mary and Martha were distraught with grief because their brother, Lazarus, died. This grief turned into fear and doubt. If only Jesus had been there, their brother would not have died. "If only" can sap the very breath from your daily life. After hearing that Lazarus had died, Jesus came two days later. He seemed unsympathetic but Jesus had a purpose. It is easy to allow the facts in your life to challenge what you believe. When Jesus shows up in your life, there will be no denying that He is the One who gave you the victory. Jesus spoke to the dead man Lazarus that day and came out of that tomb. There was no doubt that Jesus was the reason for that miracle.

What challenges are you defeating that have tried to bring fear and doubt into your life?

QUESTION TO CONSIDER: What do you do when fear knocks on your door?

> *35 While He was still speaking, some came from the ruler of the synagogue's house who said, "Your daughter is dead. Why trouble the Teacher any further?" 36 As soon as Jesus heard the word that was spoken, He said to the ruler of the synagogue, "Do not be afraid; only believe." (Mark 5:35-36)*

When tragedy strikes, it often comes without warning, crashing down on you. I believe it happened that way for Jairus, a prosperous ruler of the synagogue. This highly respected citizen of Capernaum went up to Jesus in the multitude of pushing and shoving individuals, but he was not there to pay his respects to Jesus. He was distraught and trembling as he fell on his knees before Jesus.

Jesus was Jairus' last hope.

His daughter was very ill and near death. He believed that if Jesus could touch his child, she would live. Jairus then received the message that his daughter had died. Jesus overheard the message of death and then reassured Jairus that it only took belief and his daughter would be made whole. There comes a time in our lives when even solid faith buckles. We hope against hope and then our hopes are dashed. We are tempted to give up and walk away from Jesus. But Jesus doesn't give up that easily. "Don't be afraid," He says. "Just believe." So, simple and yet so profound. Of course, Jesus came through that day and Jairus' daughter was supernaturally raised from the dead.

DAILY PRAYER: *Allow faith to accompany your prayer today.*

Lord Jesus, I give up. I realize I cannot change those circumstances that have locked me up in a prison of fear and doubt. I desire freedom more than wealth or popularity. I release faith to overcome the chains that have imprisoned me. Thank you for setting me free from condemnation and fear of the unknown. Amen.

Prayer Reflections:

_____

_____

_____

_____

_____

_____

_____

Day 26

Here Come the Dreamers

 *It's time to dream again.*

⁸ I am the Lord, that is My name; And My glory I will not give to another, Nor My praise to carved images. ⁹ Behold, the former things have come to pass, And new things I declare; Before they spring forth I tell you of them." (Isaiah 42:8-9)

THOUGHT FOR TODAY: When God is speaking, it is our responsibility to believe what He is saying.

QUESTION TO CONSIDER: What is the origin of dreams?

Each one of us can describe a season in our lives when the dreams we had were taken out of from us.

We were no longer dreamers. We wondered if our lives would ever change. Would today repeat itself over and over. We ask ourselves, "Will I have enough life left to fulfill God's purpose?" Dreams come from the God dimension. If God said it, we have to just believe it.

Many people have lost their dream and have settled into survival. I want to remind you today that dreams and visions are the blueprint that God uses to build your life. Dreams and visions are the evidence that the Holy Spirit is at work in you. The young man Joseph was called a dreamer because his dreams established his destiny.

> Then they said to one another, "Look, this dreamer is coming! (Genesis 37:19)

God gave Joseph dreams and the ability to interpret those dreams. I think Joseph would tell us that dreams are conceived long before they are achieved. Between the birth of a dream and its realization is always a process, and that period is filled with doubts, adversity, changes and even surprises. During the process, you will experience good and bad days and more often you will be faced with a dilemma, but don't give up.

Dreams were a vehicle that transported Joseph from the pit to the palace in Egypt.

When Joseph's brothers threw him into the pit, Joseph learned to submit to God. Even though your dreams do not begin well, don't give up. Joseph was young and immature while being misunderstood by his family. He was sold into slavery and forced to work in a foreign country before being thrown into prison. *Yet Joseph did not give up.* Sometimes God sends adversity to purify our motives, refine our dreams and prepare us to realize our visions. So, when you find yourself in a pit, misunderstood and mistreated, allow it to make you better not bitter.

Adversity builds character. You do not have to remain a victim of your past. The story of Joseph shows what God can do in spite of your upbringing. Because of the lies of the wife of Joseph's master, Joseph was thrown into prison, despite being innocent. Joseph learned to submit to God while in prison and had to experience thirteen years of adversity in order to be ready for momentous responsibility - to save his own people. Because Joseph was enabled by God to interpret the dreams of Pharaoh, Joseph was honored with the most senior position in Egypt.

 What dreams do you have that you have not shared with anyone?

QUESTION TO CONSIDER: How can you live instead of simply surviving?

If you are breathing, God is not through with you yet. Dreams and visions are the blueprint of the future. It takes wisdom and zeal to step into the future. Prophetic declarations of God are generational, not merely personal. It is a word that is being released into the atmosphere for a generation yet to be born. Can you now see why the devil would want to steal your dreams? Not just for you but your generations to come. The dream is what we can see about the future. The vision is the roadmap to help us get there.

Sometimes it is more important to start a movement than see it completed.

This is why you cannot lose your focus or give up on your dreams. You may be planting seeds into a future that you may not reap while you are on this earth. The Bible tells us that in the Kingdom, the last on earth shall be first in Heaven.

There is no success that does not require sacrifice. God requires fruitfulness and faithfulness. You must be willing to impact the future as well as the present. Do not live for the moment when generations to come are needing you to bank for eternity.

Determine that your life will be your children's foundation, not their ceiling.

You want those coming after you to accomplish more than you could ever achieve. Remember that you were birthed for a purpose. You don't have to go looking for it. It will come to you.

DAILY PRAYER: *Express your heart to Jesus Christ.*

Lord Jesus, I don't ask You to relieve every pain I have or am experiencing; however, I ask You to fulfill Your purpose in and through me today. Make Your dream for my life vivid in my spirit and give me the will to accomplish Your plan for my life. I decree and declare that my dreams shall come to pass through Your Holy Spirit anointing. I shall invest in generations to come. Amen.

Prayer Reflections:

_____

_____

_____

_____

_____

_____

_____

_____

_____

Day 27

Moving On

 Just because the curtain closes doesn't mean the production is over.

I can do all things through Christ who strengthens me. (Philippians 4:13)

THOUGHT FOR TODAY: You cannot go to the next level with soul ties from your past.

QUESTION TO CONSIDER: To become the master of your destiny, how can you learn to control the nature of your dominant, habitual thoughts?

One of the most important steps you can take toward achieving your greatest potential in life is to learn to monitor your thoughts and its impact on your attitude. Everything you perceive in the physical world has its origin in the invisible, inner world of your thoughts and beliefs.

Keep your heart with all diligence, for out of it spring the issues of life. (Proverbs 4:23)

Your mind is the master builder and that which you think about most of the time may become misery or miracle. Your thoughts determine your destiny. You cannot allow past relationships to determine your next steps, and yet, you must know how to find release from your soul ties. The Bible doesn't use the word *soul tie*, but it speaks of them when it talks about souls being knit together becoming one flesh. A soul tie can serve as many functions, but in its simplest form, it ties two souls together in the spiritual realm.

Soul ties between married couples draw them together like magnets, while a soul tie between two people in sin can draw an abused woman to the man which, in the natural, she would never allow to be a part of her life. However, when there is a soul tie between two people out of the sanctity of the Holy Spirit, they will run to each other, which will serve as a bridge in which to pass demonic garbage. When you have many past relationships, you may find it difficult to bond or be joined with anyone because your soul is fragmented.

"For this reason a man shall leave his father and mother and be joined to his wife, and the two shall become one flesh." (Ephesians 5:31)

The Bible shows us that Godly soul ties are formed when a couple is married. The Godly soul tie between a husband and wife, as intended by God, is unbreakable by man. Does it happen? Absolutely. There are relationships that become broken even when both spouses are "in the church." Just being a church member does not give you the guarantee that you will never face this trial; however, if you face it, you have a promise that God will never leave you.

 *Think about those relationships in your life that have negatively affected you.*

QUESTION TO CONSIDER: What steps can you take to break soul ties in your life?

God has to close the curtain to set up the stage for your next season. You cannot go to the next level with soul ties from your past. To break a soul tie in your life, you must first recognize that it is a soul tie. Then, repent for any sin that caused you to form an ungodly relationship that is affecting you negatively. You cannot break an ungodly relationship and still try to keep that person as a friend or person of influence in your life. Even rash vows or commitments made that played a part in forming the soul tie need to be renounced and repented of, and broken in Jesus' name. Even statements like, "I will always love you", or "I could never love anyone like I love you", need to be renounced.

> *Whoever guards his mouth and tongue keeps his soul from troubles. (Proverbs 21:23)*

You cannot get to your future as long as you live in your past. When you're struggling with inner secrets, God can't order your future. Stop being ruled by fear and allow your Father to elevate you to that place that He has purposed for you. Stop praying fear-based prayers and speak life where you want to go. Anyone can walk around pitiful and not powerful.

You walked through your mess for a reason.

You must walk through hell and win to allow the anointing to overtake you.

DAILY PRAYER: *Release those soul ties as you step forward.*

Lord Jesus, I realize my detours are simply Your perfect plan to get me exactly where You want me to be. I will trust You because You know the way to my destiny. I decree and declare that today is the day that I allow You to lead and guide my life. I release all relationships that are not in Your plan and give You rule and reign of my every step from this day forward. Amen.

Prayer Reflections:

_____

_____

_____

_____

_____

_____

_____

_____

_____

Day 28

Heaven Knows Your Name

 *God can take those with the worst past and give them the very best future.*

But above all these things put on love, which is the bond of perfection. (Colossians 3:14)

THOUGHT FOR TODAY: God calls us to love others based on His action on the cross.

QUESTION TO CONSIDER: What is the number one job description for a Christian?

The Bible tells us to put on love which binds everything together in perfect harmony. Because each one of us has lived in sin, we must be a reflection of God's love for one another. You may not be the people's first choice but neither was David. He was chosen by God. God develops you in the dark room of life. At one time, to develop film, which would become a beautiful photo, it had to go through several stages of development in a dark room. You can look back at the different seasons in your life and realize there were times you were in the process of going through the dark rooms of your life. Today, we live in a fast food society and want everything now; however, we must go through the dark room process with our destiny. If God has assigned you, He will find you.

When Samuel was instructed by God to anoint David as king in I Samuel 16, the anointing had left King Saul. God was ready for a change so Samuel anointed David in the midst of his entire family. The Lord has anointed you in the presence of everyone, and now you are wondering why life isn't getting easier. You can be gifted, but it's nothing without the anointing. You do not get the anointing with the crushing. You do not get the crushing without the dark room process. For David, the process was thirteen years.

> *Therefore all the elders of Israel came to the king at Hebron, and King David made a covenant with them at Hebron before the Lord. And they anointed David king over Israel. (2 Samuel 5:3)*

Anointed at age seventeen and appointed at thirty,

David's life in those thirteen years were spent in the wilderness dodging spears, being falsely accused and running from Saul. God was preparing him for development. God takes you from appointing to anointing and will give you a prophetic word for your future. I was given a prophetic word twenty-five years before I began doing what I love to do today. God had to take me through the process to prepare me. Even when I thought I was ready, God knew I did not have any idea how to discern the hurts of others as long as I was full of it myself. God had to take me through the dark room to get me free from myself. God chooses you. You do not choose your destiny.

It is easy to want to change the world and yet you haven't even gotten out of bed today. You must start where you are by getting involved in your church. God will take you through the dark room as you scrub floors, clean toilets, hold babies in the nursery or greet others on Sunday morning. I am now traveling all over the world because I allowed God to process me during humbling times. He wanted to see my actions without the cameras and large stages. If I could not handle the small, how could He trust me with my now?

What changes would you make today that can assist God in promoting you tomorrow?

QUESTION TO CONSIDER: Does God have a plan for you beyond your mistakes?

> *⁷ Where can I go from Your Spirit? Or where can I flee from Your presence? ⁸ If I ascend into heaven, You are there; If I make my bed in hell, behold, You are there. ⁹ If I take the wings of the morning, And dwell in the uttermost parts of the sea, ¹⁰ Even there Your hand shall lead me, And Your right hand shall hold me. (Psalm 139:7-10)*

As you are reading and studying today, know that it is time for you to get realigned with God's plan for your life. Sometimes you aren't going to be invited to your own party. David was the only one of Jacob's boys who wasn't invited to the anointing party. I bet David was excited there was no social media then. Many times, you break your own heart by scrolling through hash tags wondering why you aren't invited to a conference or party. David did not detest his seasons. He was faithful in each season of preparation.

You cannot receive that promotion without being faithful during your season of preparation.

You cannot be ready for the Goliath experience unless you are faithful where you are located today.

It is better to be marked by God than marketed

by man. When God marks you, no one can unmark you and when you're called, He will find, appoint, and position you. You will never need to spend time looking back when you are confident in who God has called you to be.

DAILY PRAYER: *Allow God to move you forward.*

Lord Jesus, forgive me for getting in Your way to make my own plan. I accept You in my heart. I shake off depression, defeat, hopelessness. Today I choose happiness. Today I surrender heartache and fear, and remain focused and faithful in doing Your will in my life. Lord, rule and reign today as my Savior. Amen.

Prayer Reflections:

_____

_____

_____

_____

_____

_____

_____

Day 29

A Place Called Process

| Don't be afraid to be vulnerable and transparent |

The fear of the Lord is the beginning of knowledge, But fools despise wisdom and instruction. (Proverbs 1:7)

THOUGHT FOR TODAY: Expose your scars!

QUESTION TO CONSIDER: How can you deal with process in your life so you can heal?

In process, you have to faith it when you don't feel it. There is the place for strength, but also the place for process. You must never take this for granted. When you go through due process on your journey, you become well prepared for whatever assignment God has for you. Jesus Christ went through His own process for forty days in the wilderness before completing His mission on earth.

You shall also be a crown of glory in the hand of the Lord, And a royal diadem in the hand of your God. (Isaiah 62:3)

You sing a song, *"You Make All Things New,"* and wonder the entire time why you have so many situations in your life that aren't new. Why do you think the enemy attacks you in your mind? Even the Bible tells you in Romans 12:2 to not conform to this world but be transformed by the renewing of your mind.

The enemy will imprison you in your emotions while causing you to stay bound to that impossible situation that you need to control. Before you realize it, that situation has become an idol in your life.

> *For we are His workmanship, created in Christ Jesus for good works, which God prepared beforehand that we should walk in them. (Ephesians 2:10)*

God knew the journey you would take in your process of life.

As I prayed, I asked why do so many people fail. God said, "It's not that people do not love Me. It's that their spiritual core is weak." When I gave birth to my amazing sons by C-section, I had no idea it would take my body several months to recuperate from the surgery.

My inner core needed time for recuperation because it had been weakened. Your spiritual core can also be weakened by your process; however, you can become strong in Him by allowing Him to work through you.

In Matthew 22:39, Jesus tells you to love others as yourself. The problem is if you do not love yourself, you cannot love others. We struggle to love with our broken hearts, broken souls and broken minds. It's not ironic that He starts with your heart. Passion flows from the heart, and without passion, nothing else matters.

> *Keep your heart with all diligence, for out*
> *of it spring the issues of life. (Proverbs 4:23)*

How is your passion for Jesus? If your heart is not in serving God, everything you do will become a boring obligation. When your heart becomes toxic, you are headed for a spiritual heart attack. Today ask Jesus to perform spiritual open-heart surgery on you so you can receive joy- that unspeakable joy that will last throughout your life journey.

 You can get your joy back. When your heart is in it, passion is also there.

QUESTION TO CONSIDER: How does serving Jesus affect your daily life?

You cannot be pitiful and powerful at the same

time. You see, Christianity works from the inside out and will then affect your physical man. Just because you accept Jesus as Lord does not mean you lose that weight or all your wrong decisions are made right in an instant. Jesus will work with you to lose much-needed weight and will be there as you process the losses and determine how to change your path. He is not your Santa Claus, He is your helper. The Spirit of God comes in and shines a light on those dark places in your life so you can allow Him to have an invasion within you.

In Him was life, and the life was the light of men. (John 1:4)

Everything was created by God and nothing came into being without Him. *That means you!* He needs you to allow Him to work through you as you move away from your past into healing and restoration.

You can start bad and end good!

Your past does not have to define your future. Make what Jesus did for you greater than what others have done to you. It's time for you to move on. Loving God with all your heart, soul and mind will take you to your destiny! Remind your enemies about what your Father says about you. If you are not in your word, you will not know what He says.

I will praise You, for I am fearfully and wonderfully made; Marvelous are Your works, And that my soul knows very well. (Psalm 139:14)

Daily Prayer: *Agree with Jesus as you determine your destiny.*

Lord Jesus, today I commit myself to You. I release all pain and unforgiveness so You can replace it with that peace that surpasses all understanding. I am a child of God who realizes I have failed many times but have gotten back up to seek You one more time. I know I am beautifully and wonderfully made from the inside to the outside. I shall walk out my purpose and will not allow my past to define my future. My tomorrow begins today. Amen.

Prayer Reflections:

_____

_____

_____

_____

_____

Day 30

Let It Go

*Healing is on the other side
of letting it all out!*

THOUGHT FOR TODAY: Your future is so bright!

QUESTION TO CONSIDER: How can you release the baggage that has held you hostage throughout your lifetime?

STOP letting people bring you down who have NOTHING to do with your destiny while making you emotional and distraught. People are going to talk about you till the day you die, and there is nothing you can do. So what! They don't have to like you and you don't have to care. You do you. LET IT GO! God says, "You've been in this place long enough. It's time to arise! Your breakthrough is breaking forth. There's a miracle with your name in it."

There is power in hope!

Then the word of the LORD *came to him....*
(1 Kings 17:8)

You are one word away from your miracle. When God wants to start something, He sends a word and your word is looking for you. Elijah was given a word by God to go to Zarephath because God had commanded a widow to provide for him during the famine. As he arrives, the widow is gathering sticks to cook the last meal for her and her son. She explained to the man of God that she only had enough for one last meal and then they will die.

Elijah instructed her to prepare that small meal and give it to him. Most people would be harassing the prophet for being so selfish at this time of lack however, Elijah had received a word from God. You think you are at the end of your road, but your word is walking towards you. The widow did not know that what she had left was all she needed. There are sixty-six books in the Bible, and you are book sixty-seven.

Some people will not ever read the Bible but they will read your life.

The widow was the only one out looking for sticks to prepare a meal. She was the only one who still had hope that God would provide. She obeyed the prophet and gave him all she had to eat. She was functioning in hope while knowing this was her last day of food. What she didn't know was it was her last day of impossible as she began to walk in her overflow. The widow and her household ate for many days because she accepted a word.

Later this widow's son becomes very ill until there isn't any breath left in him. As she approached the prophet, she inquired if he had come to remember her sin and kill her son. Elijah took her son to his room and cried out to God. The reason the enemy had come for her son is because he knew that her hope was in her son. The devil comes to steal, kill and destroy. Her eating wasn't the miracle. God sent this entire scenario to prepare her for her son dying.

> *God knew the enemy was coming after her legacy so he prepared her for the battle.*

Each one of us are in a battle for our legacy. When God created Adam and Eve, He wanted family. When you realize others are counting on you making it, you will then be able to rise up in the face of opposition and face your giant as you become that giant slayer.

Your life challenge is requiring preparation.

QUESTION TO CONSIDER: How can you move from where you are to where God has purposed you to be?

Never beg people to see the good in you. You just do you and let your life reveal your gift! BELIEVE in yourself. God already sees your potential! David was a young shepherd boy who waited on God to promote him to king after he was anointed. He realized he could not walk in the purpose of greatness until it was God's time!

Esther was a Gentile orphan who was raised by her uncle who waited on God to set her in position to save her people!

You cannot allow your emotions to control your destiny.

You must accept that God does have a plan and purpose already in motion before you were born. When you realize God will make a way when there seems to be none, it frees you up to be the person God created you to be. You will then have divine appointments that many times may seem like chance meetings. God uses people and circumstances to get you where you are to be. From the anxieties and turmoil that David suffered, he developed faith, resourcefulness and determination.

And when he had removed him, he raised up unto them David to be their king; to whom also he gave their testimony, and

said, I have found David the son of Jesse,
a man after mine own heart, which shall
fulfill all my will. (Acts 13:22)

God will never allow what you lost to be the best you ever had. When God sees that you appreciate your Now, He will start to release your Next! True freedom will only bloom in your life when you put on the truth of who God says you are. Remember who you are in Christ, practice being who God says you are and then step into your freedom!

DAILY PRAYER: *Release your frustrations and allow God to give you peace.*

Lord Jesus, I give up. I cannot walk without You and be all that You called me to be. I know that all things work together for the good to those who love God and to those who are called according to His purpose. You command me in Your word to not only listen, but do what it says. Today I let go of all the excess baggage and allow You to be Lord of my life. I step into my destiny as a powerful Child of the King. Amen.

Prayer Reflections:

_____

_____

_____

_____

_____

_____

_____

_____

_____

_____

_____

_____

_____

_____

_____

_____

_____

_____

_____

_____

_____

_____

_____

Day 31

It's Time to Reset

 We can't get a restart without God.

THOUGHT FOR TODAY: We all need points in life when we need a clean slate.

QUESTION TO CONSIDER: Can we get resets without God?

There are times in your life when God is guiding you to a new beginning. This time usually comes after you have felt that sin, guilt and mistakes have caused so much damage that you feel there is no way out. What I have learned is that these bad times are not the end of me -- they are my turning points to a new season. Restarts come from these turning points when you have to decide what you believe and ultimately turn back to God.

God loves restarts!

He loves restarts because they require us to turn to Him; no matter how hard we try, how much we deny, or how far we've gone, we can't get resets without God. God will never allow our hearts to stay far away from Him, so He is always working to guide us back to Him. When you begin to desire what God wants more than your own selfish desires, you will then come face to face with your turning point.

Are you needing a restart in your marriage, a new beginning in parenting or maybe a do-over in your friendships? In the book of Isaiah, the people of Israel needed a restart in their relationship with God. They had reached a turning point, and God gave them certain steps to take to return to Him.

> *Go through, Go through the gates! Prepare the way for the people; Build up, Build up the highway! Take out the stones, Lift up a banner for the peoples! (Isaiah 62:10)*

God calls us to reset by building up the road, taking out the stones and lifting up a banner for the people.

To build up or smooth out the road, faith must be the common denominator. You are never promised a path strewn with roses as you travel through this life toward your eternal purpose, however Jesus promises to never leave you nor forsake you. Through your faith, God is protecting you by His power until you hear the words, "Well done!" Even though life is tough, at times, and you face trials that you sometimes think you cannot endure, these trials will prove your genuine faith.

> *⁶ So be truly glad. There is wonderful joy ahead, even though you must endure many trials for a little while. ⁷ These trials will show that your faith is genuine. It is being tested as fire tests and purifies gold— though your faith is far more precious than mere gold. So when your faith remains strong through many trials, it will bring you much praise and glory and honor on the day when Jesus Christ is revealed to the whole world. {I Peter 1:6-8}*

In the trials of life, faith is what smoothes out the road and makes travel much easier. Faith enables you to keep going because you see God and not your circumstances. There are three specific ways faith paves the road before each of us. Faith believes God is good. Faith enables God to show you the bigger picture so you do not get stuck in the moment. Faith knows adversity will make you stronger.

In Isaiah 62:10, the second obstacle you must face is getting rid of the stones or boulders that cause aggravation. Prayer is the only thing that helps you clear out those obstacles that prevent you from changing and growing. Each of us have obstacles that hinder our growth such as unbelief, fear, mistrust and selfishness.

6 I have set watchmen on your walls, O Jerusalem; They shall never hold their peace day or night. You who make mention of the LORD, do not keep silent, 7 And give Him no rest till He establishes And till He makes Jerusalem a praise in the earth. (Isaiah 62:6-7)

Unbelief tells you that you can never change, that you'll never be fruitful, and that God no longer has a plan for your future. Fear tells you your family will never find reconciliation, you will never be able to get that promotion. Faith tells you God loves family. He will never give up on you. Faith tells you that you are fearfully and wonderfully made. The apple of God's eye!

Your life is driven by "self" sins!

QUESTION TO PONDER: How can you make your past into stepping stones for your future?

The third stone or boulder on your path to your purpose is to raise up a banner or standard before the people. Once the road is smooth and the boulders are excavated, God raises a flag for all to see. This means that everything we go through in life, the good, the bad and the ugly, is there for God to use to show people what a a mighty God we serve. I have realized that, if I do not hide in the middle of difficulty or isolate in times of challenge, my life can be a banner used by God to give hope to others.

The reason God has given me an international platform is because I choose to allow others to see my weaknesses and then share the process of how God is helping me in transition. I realize I must be an open book for others to read if I expect to walk alongside beside them in their pain and deliverance. You can never demand trust or respect. It must be earned.

After spending thirty-one days with me on my journey, I am giving you an opportunity for a restart. You now have the essential steps to change and characters in scripture who had their own restart, so it's your day to begin. How did Ruth turn her life around in the face of deep tragedy? What made Esther rise from obscurity and fear to save her nation? How did Hannah find faith in the most discouraging time of her life? Just as God chose normal people to become mighty warriors in His Word, He has chosen you to change your world! Your restart begins now!

DAILY PRAYER: *Humbly give God your present and future!*

Lord Jesus, I walk by faith and not by sight! I refuse to allow unbelief, fear, mistrust or selfishness to become a boulder in my journey. Today, I release all negative emotions and give you my all! Today is the first day of the rest of my life! Amen.

PRAYER RELECTIONS:

_____

_____

_____

_____

_____

_____

_____

_____

_____

_____

_____

_____

About the Author

Kimberly Jones-Pothier is a wife, mother, pastor, entrepreneur, best-selling author, entertainer, and worshiper after God's own heart. Pastor Kim and her husband, Mark Pothier, are the senior pastors at Church of the Harvest in Fayetteville, Georgia, and together they have four sons. In Beautifully Whole, Kim takes you on her journey to find God, her purpose, and herself as she walks you through her process of deliverance and restoration.